May this book give the
help God can give you.
William E. Crane
June 25, 1970

D1265142

WHERE GOD
COMES IN

WHERE GOD
COMES IN

The Divine "Plus" in Counseling

~~~~~~

William E. Crane

~~~~~~

WORD BOOKS, Publishers

Waco, Texas · London, England

WHERE GOD COMES IN

Printed in the United States of America.
Library of Congress Catalog Card Number: 79–111959

This book is dedicated to

God's Holy Spirit, whom it is intended to
   recognize and honor above all others for His
      presence and guidance in my counseling ministry

My wife, Katharine Rowland Crane, without
   whose love, patience, understanding, and
      valuable help it would never have been
         written

The memory of our beloved son, the Reverend
   Paul Edgar Crane, whose life was lived in the
      spirit of Christ and as His faithful servant
         and counselor until he was honored by God's
            call to a higher service on October 15, 1969

CONTENTS

PREFACE

This book was written to record some of the rich experiences that have been mine through the forty-five years of my ministry as pastor and counselor. I have done so with deep gratitude to God and to the many counselees whom it has been my privilege to serve and with whom I have shared experiences in the counseling relationship. The identities of these friends I have tried to conceal without distorting the basic facts of our relationship, since I count the confidences they have entrusted to me as sacred and private. Yet I feel it is important to give credit to them. But more important, I want to give credit to the "Wonderful Counselor" who worked in and through us to accomplish something helpful. He indeed is the divine "plus" in counseling.

I hope that this account will encourage, inspire, and guide both laymen and ministers in the vital interpersonal relationship of counseling. All of us counselors may have the immense privilege of standing at the point where God comes in—to revolutionize lives through the work of His Spirit.

WILLIAM E. CRANE

January 1970
Athens, Georgia

WHERE GOD
COMES IN

1. HUMAN NEED
AND DIVINE HELP

Being a person means needing help. I don't know of anyone who would question that statement. But do we know the relationship between our needs and God's resources and how we may draw on those resources to meet these needs? It seems to me that many of us miss this relationship; we do not know how to draw on God's resources, to find help from Him. That is my concern in this book. But first let me talk about human need.

One of our earliest and most basic needs is the need to feel secure. This includes the need for adequate provision for physical needs—food, shelter, warmth, etc.—but also it means that a child needs to feel safe and secure with his parents. Fear of separation is so frightening that it often affects a child's whole life. In my own early childhood the fear of the separation from my mother and my home when it was burned, were important enough in my early life to have had some bearing on my future.

Another illustration involves a sixty-five-year-old woman who still remembers sixty years later her feeling of anxiety when her mother left her, in perfectly good and loving hands, to go with her father to the World's Fair in another city. Her memory is even more vivid because her older brother pulled her hair, generally irritated her, and locked her up in a chicken house. She was so young and so small that she escaped by crawling through the opening where the hens entered.

In my files is still another incident which had a much more lasting and negative effect upon the child's development. When Anna was eighteen months old (substantiated in the counseling procedure by checking with her parents), her mother put her in her crib, told her to go to sleep and be quiet, and left her in her room with the door closed. While her mother was out of the room, Anna saw a reflection in the mirror at the foot of the bed of a frightening image which she could not understand, and screamed for help. Her mother rushed in, but not finding any reason for Anna's fright, spanked her, warned her to be quiet, and went out and closed the door again. The long-range result was Anna's genuine dislike and hostility toward her mother which lingered up to her teenage years. Although it showed itself in many forms, it was particularly evident in Anna's finding countless ways to embarrass her mother and to cause her anxiety.

In the first two instances apparently no permanent or serious damage was done. Probably the reason was that in each of these homes there was a strong emphasis on family prayers and the presence and love of God in the home. In the last instance, however, the child's insecurity was deepened because there was a strong sense of insecurity on the mother's part. She always feared that she would not measure up to her own standards or to the standards of other mothers. Whenever her children did not measure up to her image of proper performance, she felt she would be criticized as being inadequate as a mother.

As a child grows and enters school, the same need for security continues, but now there are other figures besides the parents who enter the scene. School teachers, Sunday school teachers, peer groups, and others contribute either to a sense of security or to a sense of insecurity.

I recall several instances where a young grade-school child was made to feel insecure by some word or action on the part of a teacher or some other person. John, for example, was called up before his third-grade class by his teacher and given a sound switching for chewing gum. He felt so mistreated and rejected that throughout the rest of his school years he found it extremely difficult to stand up before a class to answer questions or do anything that might possibly bring laughter or embarrassment from his fellows or a scolding from his teacher.

Another illustration involves Mark who had two older brothers, one of whom was extremely bright and made excellent grades at school. The other made very good grades, though with not quite such a high average. Whether or not it was intentional on the part of the family, the boy who made the high grades seemed to get the greatest amount of attention and praise. Mark felt he was under great pressure to measure up in order to gain the recognition and approval he needed from his family. The effect of this pressure continued in his subconscious mind and followed him into adulthood. Because he was never able to measure up to the standards which his older brother had set, he still felt inadequate and unaccepted by his family even when he was in his late fifties.

Had Mark's family, some friend, or other person been able to reassure him of his worth and importance in the sight of God, he would not have needed to compare his achievements with his brother or any other person. His whole life might have been different and much more effective.

Many children find this a real problem. They feel they are in competition with a brother or sister for the attention, affection, and approval of the parents because of their educational achievements. Surely parents need to be made aware of such possibilities, so that they will give more adequate attention and approval to the efforts of each of their children. We are all born with varying abilities and capacities. Parents certainly need to recognize this fact and become mature and secure enough within themselves to accept variations among their children and limitations on the part of some. They need not feel that they have failed if some of their children do not make the highest grades.

How do the resources of God meet the needs of insecure people—whether parents or children? Perhaps the basic need is for each person to know personally the presence, power, and attitude of God in His Holy Spirit.

It is really not enough for a developing child to be told that God is love, and that God is everywhere. These statements are beyond his comprehension, for he cannot see God or hear Him speak. A child is confined to the realm of the senses, and abstract words tend to be meaningless. "Seeing is believing" seems to be inherent in human beings. Only a genuine and convincing type of religious education will expand into reality that which is not within the realm of the senses.

It is possible to teach a child that all things do not have to be seen in order to be accepted. Parents and counselors can use analogies with which children are familiar, such as that of the invisible and effective power of electricity, or the necessity for oxygen which is not seen but which is inhaled for our very existence. The Scriptures teach clearly that God is not far removed from us as if in a remote kingdom upon some distant throne; He has come into this world as a human being; but more, He wishes to enter into and actually live within each one of us in a form described as "spiritual." Although "spirit" is intangible and invisible, it is capable of being accepted as a reality.

In today's world there are vast opportunities for teaching the reality of the intangible and invisible spiritual factor in our lives. We experience the mystery and wonder of the radio which brings to us voices from any part of the world. We see the marvel of television which brings pictures and voices into our living rooms of actions taking place at that very moment across the wide expanse of oceans or of space. We say to the child, "We can't see radio or television waves, but we know they must be there since by some means these pictures and voices are brought to us on our television."

The earliest record of an analogy to describe the nature of the spiritual is given in the second verse of the first book in the Bible. Here in Genesis 1:2 we have the words, "The Spirit of God was moving over the face of the waters." The Hebrew word which we translate "spirit" is the same word which is used elsewhere for "air, breath, or wind." Each one of these words is familiar even to a small child and can wisely and intelligently be used to help him understand the nature of that which we speak of as "spirit" or "spiritual."

I have also found the analogy of these words useful in helping adults to recognize the reality and presence of God in our society. Each of the three words can be elaborated on for illustration. For example, the Scripture says of God, "In him we live and move and have our being." How can this be when we speak of God as a person and use the personal pronoun "Him"? The answer must be in the mystery of God's spiritual nature, and here the analogy of air is a convenient one to use.

We know that man must live in an atmosphere which contains oxygen; we call this atmosphere in our common language "air." If air is removed from the room in which we are, then we cannot live or move, for oxygen is absolutely essential to our existence. Wherever we go we must remain within the confines of the "air."

So it is with God. Because He is spirit (in the nature of air) we cannot live or move apart from Him. It is in His presence that we exist, and only in His presence that we can exist and do the things which we are able to do. The physical effects of removing the oxygen or air from our environment are good illustrations of the necessity and reality of God's presence.

When the air in a room lacks sufficient oxygen, the mind

becomes dim and the thought-life foggy. This is accompanied by depression and anxiety, and eventually leads to a desperate effort to let in the oxygen from outside. We become panicky when we cannot have enough oxygen for the restoration of our depleted mind and body.

The wise parent or counselor can use this analogy quite effectively in helping a child or counselee to understand and accept the necessity for an intimate relationship with God and the recognition of our need for Him every hour.

The next word in our Old Testament analogy is equally helpful in understanding the nature of God—the word "breath." Breath is different from air, and yet related to it; one must breathe in order to inhale the oxygen which is so essential for existence. To a degree, breathing is involuntary and compulsive, but at times it may become controlled and voluntary. A child may by his own will "hold his breath." This of course means that he refuses to breathe—to receive the oxygen or to exhale the carbon dioxide which is debilitating and poison to his system. If he refuses to breathe long enough or when he allows any obstruction to prevent him from breathing, the child will die.

Apparently the figure holds true of the nature of the spirit and especially of God the Holy Spirit in His relationship to us. We are told that we may voluntarily "resist" the Holy Spirit, or that we may refuse or reject Him. To do so, however, is as deadly to the spiritual life as the child's refusal to breathe is to his physical life.

This analogy brings a new responsibility to the parent or counselor if he would make the child or counselee aware of the presence and need of the Holy Spirit. This brings into play the matter of the exercise of one's own will. One must "decide" whether or not he will receive the Holy Spirit. The counselor needs to recognize that there may be many blocks or obstructions to a person's ability to receive the Spirit, and that these need to be removed if he is to become aware of and able to rely upon the presence and power of the Holy Spirit within his life. Doubts, fears, rebellion, and anxiety may be factors which will stand between the person and this understanding acceptance.

We must also consider the third analogy for the Spirit—the "wind." No adult or child can see wind, but we can feel it and see its powerful effects as it sways great oaks or, in its more violent form, sweeps away houses or complete towns or villages. To believe that there is a tremendous power which we call wind does not demand at the same time that we "see" the wind. By its results we recognize and admit its presence and its power.

There are innumerable instances of the powerful working of the Spirit of God in changing the lives of men from a static to an active existence. The New Testament, especially the book of the Acts of the Apostles, gives abundant evidence of this. But we do not have to confine ourselves to the Scriptures for illustrations. Biographies and autobiographies of innumerable religious and social leaders in history reveal that they could never have accomplished the things they did except for the motivation and power of some Unseen Force within them. Handicapped persons like Helen Keller are demonstrations of the ability of this Unseen Power to use one who is willing and eager to be used.

If there is such a power as the Holy Spirit, and if the word "holy" means "that which is good and acceptable," then one may believe that this powerful Spirit of goodness can change the environment in which a troubled person lives.

Countless times in my experience I have seen the whole atmosphere of a family and home change by the working of the Holy Spirit when the counselor was able to introduce the counselees to His presence and power. I have seen couples with such hostility toward each other that they could not sit in the same room or have a joint interview without the expression of anger and hate. But then as time went on and the counseling became effective in the spiritual realm, husband and wife have become more calm and willing to look objectively at the causes of certain effects which were resented in the other. Hatred has been turned to love, and fear changed into trust. By the power of the Holy Spirit working in the minds and hearts of the counselees, fear has vanished and calmness and peace have taken its place.

A study of the word "holy" as applied to spirit leads me to believe that the Holy Spirit is capable of working in counselees to accomplish everything that could be desired by a counselor who has genuine concern for the growth and maturity of those who come to him with problems.

In my own personal experience, the first lesson I was taught by my parents about God came in the teaching of the simple statement, "God is everywhere." As time went on and my mind became more acquisitive, I searched in the Scriptures to see what they had to say about this. Again and again I found reassurances both in the narrative stories of the lives of men and women and in the forthright statements made which demonstrated this truth.

In my adolescent period of stress and struggle one verse from Matthew stood out very strongly in my mind and became a stabilizing factor. "Lo, I am with you alway, even unto the end of the world" (28:20, KJV). Closely associated with this verse was another, "I will never leave thee, nor forsake thee" (Heb. 13:5, KJV). I also remember reading that "when my mother and my father forsake me, then the Lord will take me up" (Psa. 27:10, KJV). These statements tied in with my natural need for and sense of security with my parents. Here was abundant assurance that I need never feel insecure, for there is a "Heavenly Father" whose spiritual form is always present wherever I go. In His spiritual form and nature, He is just as real, essential, present, and important to me as air, breath, or wind.

How fortunate we are if the spiritual atmosphere in which we live, this aspect of God which we speak of as "Holy Spirit," is actually a "holy" atmosphere! One of the basic meanings of the word holy is "perfectly whole." Applied to the state of mind and body it would mean "sound or unimpaired" in health —or "perfection."

Such "perfection" is the ideal which is the essence of "maturity." One of the basic goals of counseling is to help a person grow from immaturity toward maturity. If one of the purposes of God's presence with us is to provide an atmosphere which is conducive to growth toward maturity—soundness of physical, mental, and spiritual health—then it would seem that the Holy Spirit should be both interested and involved in the process of counseling, and the ever-present companion and guide of the counselor.

It is wonderful to realize that God's highest purpose and intent for His children is that they constantly grow toward maturity and wholeness of character as well as of mind and body. In the person of His Holy Spirit He has provided us with the essential guide and assistance toward achieving this end. As a counselor I am comforted to realize that I am not working alone even when faced with seemingly impossible barriers in a counseling situation. When that realization strikes me, I have said to counselees, "Though I may not know the answers, I am in partnership with one who does," and I have often referred to the Holy Spirit as "the Senior Counselor" in my service of counseling.

This statement has little or no meaning to a person who is not religiously oriented. But when it is said in sincerity and not in an overly pious or artificial tone of voice, it can be extremely meaningful to a religiously oriented person. Later I shall be dealing with specific cases where I discovered the presence and work of the Holy Spirit in the counselee, and we were able to cooperate in our counseling process toward bringing about amazing changes in the counselee.

Let me summarize the ideas of the chapter in this way: All people today have one basic need—that is to recognize and accept the reality, presence, and power of God in spiritual form.

(I use the term "spiritual form," because no other form is capable of performing in, around, and through individual persons.)

Then, too, intelligent and practical people need to be presented with these facts in a rational and understandable way if they are to accept them. I have tried to do this by using the shades of meaning given to the words translated "spirit" in the original Hebrew and Greek forms. Both the Hebrew *ruach* and the Greek *pneuma* are best understood as meaning that "spirit" or "spiritual" is of the nature of "air, breath, wind." Air, breath, and wind are understandable both by a little child as well as by the most sophisticated adult. The possible ramifications and implications of these words may be pursued profitably by anyone, and such pursuit will only deepen, strengthen, and enrich our understanding of the reality of God's Spirit working in and around and through us.

Whatever other needs we may have—and all of us have plenty of them—I believe our most important and vital need is for the actualization of God's presence in the Holy Spirit. Our scientific age should make this actualization easier and more acceptable than any period in human history. As a great thinker said some years ago, "The greatest area of unexplored knowledge today is the spiritual realm." And I might add, the most needed exploration of our day is the quest for and discovery of the presence of God in the form of His Holy Spirit. For troubled man and concerned counselor, this is a "must"!

2. THE COUNSELOR
NEEDS HELP

ⓍⒾⒾⒾⒾⒾⒾⒾⒾⒾⒾⒾⒾⒾⒾⒾⒾⒾⒾⒾⒾⒾⒾⒾⒾⒾⒾⒾⓍ

The last chapter introduced us both to the pervasive needs of every person, and to the resources of God in His Holy Spirit which can meet those needs. Many people, however, are not able to make contact with God's resources on their own. They need help—some person to confront them with their needs and to teach them about God. This is where the human counselor comes in—the pastor or Christian leader who knows both human (his own) weakness and God's grace and strength through the Holy Spirit.

In his book, *Basic Types of Pastoral Counseling,* Dr. Harold Clinebell makes this statement: "The effectiveness of any form of pastoral counseling will always be contingent on one factor —the pastor himself. To the degree that he is open, genuine, free, self-accepting, and growing, he will naturally foster these qualities in others, even if his counseling methodology is inadequate."[1] Dr. Clinebell also quotes C. G. Jung's *Psychological*

[1] Nashville: Abingdon Press, 1966, pp. 37–38.

Reflections, as saying, "Learn your theories as well as you can, but put them aside when you touch the miracle of the living soul. Not theories but your own creative individuality alone must decide."

Many excellent volumes and articles have been written to help the pastor in increasing his skills as a pastoral counselor. Recognizing the tremendous importance and value of these and of every suggestion contained in them, I nevertheless feel that additional help of a very basic nature is needed which will increase a pastor's skills as counselor.

According to Dr. Clinebell, "There are five types of experiences which provide, in varying degrees, the deeper self-encounter which accelerates the counselor's growth: personal psychotherapy, clinical pastoral training, supervision of one's counseling, sensitivity training groups, and reality-practice" (p. 298). This self-encounter is essential to a pastor's effectiveness as a counselor.

Although these five experiences are comprehensive, I feel that more emphasis should be given to one aspect of training which every pastor has access to—an awareness of and dependence upon the Holy Spirit as the Wonderful Counselor. This awareness may, but does not necessarily, come with the experiences Dr. Clinebell describes. Some counselors who could not be called "pastoral" may achieve a high degree of efficiency through these five experiences, and yet lack to a large degree any reliance upon the Holy Spirit as the Wonderful Counselor.

My purpose in this book is to expand the opportunities for the average pastor or counselor to grow in self-awareness and self-acceptance, even though he may not have access to the five experiences Clinebell mentions. I am thinking particularly of the pastor who, because of his location geographically and his condition financially, may not be able to participate in regular and extensive personal psychotherapy, clinical pastoral training, supervision of his counseling, or sensitivity training groups. I believe that any pastor anywhere could make use of what Cline-bell calls "reality-practice."

However, I want to make it perfectly clear that I do not regard specialized training as unnecessary or dispensable. The need for a deepened awareness of and a reliance upon the Holy Spirit is not a mere substitute for any of the five experiences. But in the absence of opportunities for training, I believe a pastor may still gain many of these values from a concentration upon and fellowship with the Holy Spirit in his study and in his parish.

Before the days of psychotherapists or psychiatrists or clinical training and clinical supervisors, there were many effective counselors, the record of whose lives is available to anyone who makes himself familiar with the literature of biography, autobiography, and Scripture.

In primitive times recorded in the Scripture, many persons were able to help others through direct experience with and confrontation by the Holy Spirit. Sometimes this experience came in what we think of as a miraculous or supernatural form. Sometimes it came as a result of a personal crisis or traumatic experience, as for instance when David, the adulterous murderer, was confronted by Nathan the prophet.

The depth of personal awareness and insight which came to David following his adultery with Uriah's wife and his issuing royal orders to place Uriah in the front ranks of battle so that he would be killed was an experience never to be forgotten. It changed David's whole life and made him far more capable of being a "pastoral counselor" than he could ever have been had he not had this confrontation.

Through some of his psalms, like the 32nd or the 51st, David has touched many hearts and brought awareness to countless lives. I attribute this effectiveness to the direct operation of the Holy Spirit through a man named Nathan.

I am concerned lest busy pastors of our time become so

involved in the technicalities and theories of counseling which come to us through other helping professions, that they overlook or never become aware of the Source from which all such helpfulness comes—God himself. The pastor must not forget the agent through whom God brings about this depth training in the individual's heart and thus better prepares him to counsel others. It is important and urgent to glorify God above men, however wise and helpful in their writings or their service the men may be. I dare to believe that only as we truly glorify God in our pastoral counseling ministry can we enjoy Him and enjoy also a degree of effectiveness and success. So let us focus more directly at this point upon the relationship of the counselor to the Holy Spirit in the developing of that degree of mature personality which will best enable him to function as a servant of God and of his fellow men.

Pastors learning to counsel have sought help from every source available—particularly psychology, psychiatry, and sociology. Since both college and seminary training were usually focused on either a general background of learning or a theological specialization, it is possible that we came to our counseling ministry feeling ill-prepared to understand what psychology, psychiatry, and sociology had to teach us about the inner workings and interpersonal relationships of human beings. Many of us, therefore, have felt that we must concentrate on gaining this more specialized knowledge as thoroughly and as rapidly as possible. In doing so we may have found that any one of these avenues of learning could consume most or all of our time. We may also have neglected the value of our theological training and failed to learn how it can be integrated into the field of counseling.

We do not always take the time to see how clinical training, psychotherapy, sociology, etc., relate to our theological foundations, nor do we translate our theological terminology into psychological or sociological terms so that we may be understood by these disciplines. In seeking to understand them, we may have failed to supply them with the reservoir of theological resources which might have enabled them to do more effective counseling or psychotherapy. I hope in this book to bring more of this relationship into focus and to make some contribution from the spiritual realm to that of the psychological and social approaches.

It is not always easy to translate the familiar or trite phraseology we have inherited from our religious environment into terms that are adequately and appropriately related to the other humanities. In my attempt to do this I may tend to oversimplify some of the terminology familiar to these other disciplines to fit them into my own concepts. I feel, however, that it is worth the risk—and it is a risk for a person trained in one discipline to attempt to interpret his discipline to outsiders or to define other disciplines in his own vocabulary. I shall concentrate on my own approach as pastoral counselor and hope that the insights will be useful in other disciplines.

I hope that every pastor who counsels will have the opportunity to undergo psychotherapy, which helps to remove his own psychological and emotional blocks. As long as these blocks or blind spots remain, the pastor is to that degree less effective as a counselor.

It is extremely difficult, even impossible, for a person to look at himself as he really is. Even the reflections of his personality that come from his wife or other members of his family are necessarily colored by the intimate relationships and emotions within the family circle. The desire to be helpful rather than hurtful, to be approving rather than critical, may outweigh a desire to confront him with the reality he needs to face. Therefore, a person needs to talk with someone outside the family circle, even outside his circle of intimate friends and acquaintances, if he wants to know himself more truly. If a psychotherapist or trained psychological counselor is not within the geographical or financial reach of a pastor, he must strive even harder to recognize the reality, personality, and presence of the

Holy Spirit and must rely upon Him largely to be his counselor.

The Holy Spirit has access to all the materials that other psychotherapists know and use; in addition He has direct access to the inner thoughts and feelings of the counselee. When the counselor becomes counselee in the presence of the Wonderful Counselor and sincerely seeks the honest reproval, correction, and training in righteousness which the Holy Spirit promises, then he may find it; many have.[2]

This is not to say, of course, that we are to disregard or refuse to use the human counselors who have specialized in psychotherapy, psychiatry, or psychology; for surely these become effective agents of the Holy Spirit through whom He speaks and operates in many cases. But when access to such human aids seems impossible or remote, one need not despair of gaining insight and awareness of his emotional blocks, nor need he hopelessly resign himself to continuing under his inhibitions and handicaps because he cannot receive outside specialized help.

Let me share my own experience with you. Born late in the last century, I grew up in a small town in Mississippi, far removed from the great eastern centers of higher learning. I was born into a Christian home, however, and my parents were well adjusted and farsighted. My training and development in the local school, Sunday school, and church, as well as in the home, were strong in their emphasis upon a Christian faith and its importance in human development.

Through the example and influence of the adults in my life, I became aware quite early that I had many inhibitions and fears, and I longed for relief from these. I took every opportunity possible to talk about such fears with my seniors, teachers, and parents, as well as with my peer group. But each of these contacts, while providing some help, fell short of reaching the deeper areas of my inner selfhood. I did, however, learn from

[2] II Timothy 3:16, 17.

the examples and teachings of some of these persons the value, importance, and presence of the Holy Spirit as the great teacher and Wonderful Counselor.

When I found myself faced with some frightening experience or some strong temptation to run away from reality, I often sought refuge behind the closed doors of my room at home. There, with Bible open and heart even more opened, I asked for wisdom from on high.

Increasingly I became aware not only of my need, limitations, and weaknesses, but also of the presence and power of the Holy Spirit. I came to know Him as the One who confronted me with the true nature of my weaknesses and was capable of providing help for my need. Along with confrontation, I learned that there was forgiveness and acceptance on the part of God through contact with His Spirit.

As the years went by, my interest in science as well as religion grew steadily more intense, and I pursued both fields in so far as I was able to do so in my small world. When I reached college, I was determined to get a better understanding of myself and others as well as of the world in which I lived, and so I chose to major in psychology and took courses in sociology. I also spent many hours in "bull sessions" in the fraternity hall and with my roommate. But superficial discussions did not satisfy me—I always sought that realm of reality which could meet and satisfy my deeper needs.

As time went on, I felt definitely led to seek training in theology. I wanted to understand more fully the resources available in religion. In my three years of seminary, in stress and struggle as well as in study, I tried to relate the offerings of psychology and sociology to those of theology. In and out of the classroom, I welcomed every opportunity to gain a better understanding of myself.

Sometimes these experiences were almost traumatic. Being sensitive and aware of my limitations I was easily hurt by criticism, no matter how kindly it was phrased. But I continued seeking. One experience came in a class on public speaking which I had chosen to take because I wanted to learn to speak effectively in public—something I found extremely difficult. I was assigned a reading to study and to give aloud in the class the next day. Eager to avoid as much criticism as possible, I worked for many hours on these few paragraphs, hoping to read them effectively and satisfactorily. But the next day, I had hardly read a sentence before the professor leaped to his feet and exclaimed, "Stop, stop! You haven't one bit of imagination!" I was both embarrassed and humiliated. Yet the experience was necessary to shake me out of my superficial idea that I could easily master speaking in the presence of others.

I often remembered that painful experience and also the counsel which followed it—"Read poetry! read poetry! read poetry!" I did read poetry over and over again, and in doing so developed the imagination which the professor said I totally lacked.

Years in the ministry and in the pulpit became increasingly meaningful to me and to my parishioners, for I learned to use imagination and develop it so that I could sense the feelings as well as the needs of my fellow men. Because many of them realized this, they came to me for counseling. Still seeking help, I read what books I could, listened to lectures, and spent much time in prayer that the Holy Spirit would teach me to be a more effective counselor.

I have been privileged to receive professional counseling training, but I have also become convinced, through experience, of human limitations in the deeper areas of counseling. Working with people from all walks of life and in all emotional conditions I have found myself forced constantly to supplement the best-known methods and techniques in pastoral counseling with the "cry for help from the Spirit of God." This help was so available and forthcoming that I was convinced that I must record its availability for the encouragement and guidance of others.

3. ESTABLISHING
AN EMPATHETIC RELATIONSHIP

∞∞∞∞∞∞∞∞∞∞∞∞∞∞∞∞∞∞∞∞∞∞∞∞∞∞∞∞∞∞∞∞∞∞∞∞∞∞

The person who practices the presence of the Holy Spirit and learns to love God through focusing upon His demonstration of love in the gift of His only Son becomes increasingly mature and capable of ministering to the needs of others. As Dr. Reuel Howe and others have said, nothing will take the place of love in the heart of the counselor for his counselee. This love is best defined and illustrated in the Greek word *agape* which is used in the New Testament for God's love and Christ's love for us. It is the ideal love which husbands and wives ought to have for each other.[1]

This kind of love is more concerned with giving than with getting; it is the basic factor in establishing an empathetic relationship between counselor and counselee. True empathy must have its roots in *agape* love, for only this kind of self-giving concern is capable of entering into the deeper areas of

[1] Ephesians 5:25; John 3:16; Galatians 2:20.

the counselee's problems. Lacking this basic love, a counselor may fall into the bad habit of probing and becoming too inquisitive. He may ask questions which the counselee may interpret as "too personal" or "none of his business."

But the counselor who genuinely cares, in the sense that he has Christlike love for all the people who come to him, will be able best to listen with his heart and therefore respond truthfully. Such interest and concern will foster empathy, not destroy it. A counselor may have thorough knowledge of all the techniques in counseling and a great desire to be an effective counselor, but if he lacks this "larger love," as one of my counselees called it, he will fail. There is no substitute—not even the best clinical training can take the place of a genuine concern for people in need.

It is especially urgent at this point that the importance of a vital knowledge and relationship with the Holy Spirit is seen. One cannot "learn" to love in this way through reading or academic training. A person can only achieve a genuine *agape* love through contact and fellowship with the Source of such love—God. And this contact and fellowship is possible through the presence and power of the Holy Spirit within us.

Where this vital relationship is a reality in the counselor, the "larger love" becomes the normal and inevitable fact. There can be no mistaking of the presence of *agape* love, for it always "goes out" with that warmth and genuineness which draws others into relationship and results in healing and growth otherwise impossible.

For a better understanding of the meaning of this "larger love" in empathy, let me quote from J. B. Phillips' translation of I Corinthians 13:4–8:

> This love of which I speak is slow to lose patience—it looks for a way of being constructive. It is not possessive: it is neither anxious to impress nor does it cherish inflated ideas of its own importance.
> Love has good manners and does not pursue selfish advantage.

It is not touchy. It does not keep account of evil or gloat over the wickedness of other people. On the contrary, it is glad with all good men when truth prevails.

Love knows no limit to its endurance, no end to its trust, no fading of its hope; it can outlast anything. It is, in fact, the one thing that still stands when all else has fallen.

In this description of the basic source from which empathy must spring, *agape* love, we can see the necessary characteristics of a good relationship between counselor and counselee.

First of all, there can be no empathy when one loses patience quickly with a troubled person. This can happen when one is more concerned about his own affairs than about his counselee's interests or needs. Lack of patience may destroy any possibility of empathy; it can easily be detected by the counselee whether through words or through actions and attitudes.

Sometimes the counselor shows his impatience by "pushing" the counselee too fast to get on with his problem, so that, presumably, the counselor may begin *his* "important work." The love which is basic to empathy, however, "looks for a way of being constructive." That is, the counselor with *agape* love is always seeking ways to be helpful to the other person, rather than trying to be "possessive" either of the counselee or of the time allotted for the interview. Love will prevent the counselor from being "anxious to impress" and will keep his focus on the counselee, thus avoiding the danger of cherishing "inflated ideas of his own importance."

Love also "has good manners and does not pursue selfish advantage." Courtesy is the very essence of good counseling, and the discourteous counselor does not establish or maintain empathy. Discourtesy is actually a disregard for a person's personality and rights as an individual. It is ill manners to show a lack of proper respect for the sacredness of the counselee's selfhood. No matter what techniques or words the counselor may employ, they will not be convincing in an uncomfortable atmosphere created by the ill-mannered counselor.

Pursuing selfish advantage is also part of being discourteous and ill-mannered. It automatically obscures or eliminates the possibility of genuine concern for or interest in the counselee's difficulties and needs.

The basic love from which empathy springs "is not touchy." "Touchy" implies a degree of oversensitivity on the part of the counselor, which really means that he is more concerned about receiving the counselee's praise and approval than he is of giving his attention to the counselee's needs. Here is an area where lack of insight and failure to be aware of the counselor's own emotional blocks may cause trouble and destroy empathy or make it impossible to establish empathy in the first place.

A touchy counselor is one who listens primarily for things that might reflect upon his own character or worth rather than seeking for constructive ways to be helpful to the counselee. A neurotic counselor is inclined to become extremely touchy and to be thrown on the defensive by any slight, word, or act on the part of the counselee which would insinuate that the counselor is not as important as the counselee.

Love also refuses "to keep an account of evil or gloat over the wickedness of other people." Here is an important factor for the pastoral counselor to remember. He has been taught that when he is preaching he is "speaking for God." In this role he may at times become quite judgmental, pointing out the faults and failures, sins and weaknesses of his parishioners. This is a genuine part of his preaching role, for he must direct some of his preaching toward producing in his parishioners a sense of sin and guilt and thus call them to repentance.

Though the counseling relationship may lead the counselee to become aware of his own faults and sins and the need for repentance, that is not the primary purpose of counseling. Such an awareness is only a by-product after empathy is established. The counselee must be able to rely on the counselor to be accepting and loving toward him even in his sinfulness and weakness. To be empathetic, the counselor must accept the counselee in his struggle and need; he cannot feel that he must sit in judgment upon him. The counselor, through the establishing of empathy, seeks to help the counselee not only to become aware of the causes of his problem but also to discover their solution and cure.

Rather than having a judgmental attitude, the counselor is "glad with all good men when truth prevails." This is to say that the counselor is responsive to the counselee wherever he sees in him potential for good and evidence of truth. The counselor's joy is a contributing factor in the deepening and strengthening of empathy.

There is an ongoingness in love which "knows no limit to its endurance." The counselor must learn to endure all sorts of things in his counselees. These are not always simple matters. Some counselees are very difficult to endure because of certain unpleasant mannerisms or forms of expression. The depressed person who constantly repeats the details of sadness is not easy to endure. The counselee who is excessively anxious over unimportant matters is a trial to one's endurance. Certainly the person who expresses hostility and harshness toward his mate or toward the counselor requires the counselor's endurance to the "nth" degree.

Toward all these things which are unattractive or even threatening in his counselees, the counselor must develop a higher threshold of tolerance. He must be able to endure whatever the counselee may say or do, no matter how unpleasant or threatening it may be.

But the next factor is even more difficult at times. Love knows "no end to its trust." Every counselor and especially every pastoral counselor has people who come to him clothed in hypocrisy, insincerity, and falsehood. Their neurotic problem makes them need to test the sincerity of the pastoral counselor by their very insincerity.

The smiling face, smooth words, and overly pious attitude which some counselees bring to their counseling relationship with their pastors may be deceptive for a while. Eventually the real nature is discovered—and then the counselor has a real problem. He needs to trust his counselee, but how can he trust one who is so false, deceptive, and insincere?

Actually he cannot. Nevertheless he must learn to trust his belief in and knowledge of his counselee's need for help. Above this he must have an unfailing trust in the presence and power of the Wonderful Counselor, the Holy Spirit, who is ready and willing to change the counselee from an untrustworthy person to a person of integrity and honor, through the instrument of the counselor. This basic personality change is impossible without the work of the Holy Spirit within the heart, but the pastoral counselor need never doubt it is an unfailing possibility and a desirable result in the counseling relationship.

The moment the counselor shows a lack of trust in his counselee he breaks the spirit of empathy and eliminates the possibility of being helpful. This does not mean that the counselor becomes gullible or that he is called upon to believe the unbelievable things which the counselee says or does; but he must never communicate to the counselee a lack of *faith in him as a person.* Every counselee is potentially capable of becoming an honest and trustworthy person.

Empathy needs more than trust, however. The counselor must maintain "hope" of finding answers to questions, solutions to problems, and healing for the emotionally or mentally ill person. In love there is "no fading of its hope."

I can recall many instances in my counseling ministry when hope grew very dim and almost faded. One was the case of a counselee who said that he was a homosexual. I had read in secular literature the belief of some authorities that the homosexual is incurable—perhaps the best one can do for him is to help him to accept his homosexuality as "a way of life."

In the months and years of our weekly interviews, it was a real temptation to both of us to lose hope. Living in an environment where homosexuality was not tolerated, the counselee was repeatedly rebuffed, criticized, and brought to the point of near starvation because people would not employ him. I often had to pray for the faith and courage to maintain the counselee's hope as well as my own; on every hand the circumstances of life seemed to be in opposition to this hope.

But I did manage to trust in the Holy Spirit as Counselor and in the counselee as a person worthy of time and attention. And gradually I was relieved of my fear of failure. The counselee's faith in God became so vital that he learned to endure and to love as only a Christian can. The change in his whole view of life—from fear and hostility to hope and love—was of major importance in his healing. Gradually he became so secure in his faith that he was able to go back into the very location where his weakness had been discovered and where he was forced to leave the ministry. There he was reinstated and reordained on the basis of his now mature and healed personality.

In working with this case I discovered that the Holy Spirit worked indirectly through other relationships as well as directly with the counselor and counselee. After several years of work with this man I was able to talk to two outstanding authorities on counseling the homosexual. With the permission of the counselee, I shared the case with them at an evening meal. And I found that the counselee was not really a homosexual but a bisexual. There is a tremendous difference in the prognosis given to bisexuals. These two specialists, on the basis of the case history and development, assured me that this man had risen above his difficulty and was now prepared to undertake responsibilities from which he had been expelled when discovered in a homosexual act years before.

A counselor who has *agape* love and who spends years in pastoral counseling can truthfully say that this love "can outlast anything." Though there have been many disappointments and apparent failures in my counseling ministry, I have steadily grown in my faith that love casts out fear in both counselor and counselee. Faith, hope, and love are indeed the three great virtues of the Christian faith, and all are essential to a successful counseling ministry. When we are caught up in the love of God as we see it demonstrated on Calvary's cross, we gradually reach the point where we can say from experience, love "is . . . the only thing that still stands when all else is fallen."

Two thousand years ago the writer of this letter to the Corinthians was able to express a basic fact and principle which we are now emphasizing—that the Holy Spirit as Counselor is capable of working in and through the life of an individual to bring about this more mature love, to enable him to empathize.

The closing words of I Corinthians 13 are very significant. "At present we are men looking at puzzling reflections in a mirror. The time will come when we shall see reality whole and face to face! At present all I know is a little fraction of the truth, but the time will come when I shall know it as fully as God now knows me!" (vs. 12, Phillips).

This is a very exciting statement coming from the mind and heart of Paul who, without modern conveniences and scientific knowledge, has become one of the great understanders of human nature. He has empathized with people of all races and religions and has aided them in finding the source of strength which is in Christ.

It was only by the direct inspiration of the Holy Spirit that Paul was able to see and express these facts so clearly, and they apply just as truly today. As pastoral counselors, we are men "looking at puzzling reflections in a mirror." But faith and hope and love are given to us by God through the demonstration of His unspeakable love in Christ, and they are communicated and interpreted to us by the Wonderful Counselor, His Holy Spirit. So we may have confidence that growth toward personal maturity and toward efficiency and effectiveness as counselors is a certainty, a promise to those who put their trust in Him.

God's help, of course, does not eliminate the study of the techniques and approaches in the counseling process, nor does it do away with the hard work of developing better understanding of ourselves and of others. It does provide courage and a challenge to all of us, especially where we feel cut off from many of the scientific and technical sources of assistance.

"Three things block the counselor's sensitivity to counselee feelings," says Dr. Clinebell. "Overconcern with personality theories and counseling techniques, premature attempts to think of 'solutions,' and anxiety which produces unawareness of feelings—one's own and the counselee's. Inexperienced counselors need to be encouraged to avoid trying to 'cure' the person or to find answers to his problems, and instead to concentrate on understanding the person and his world."[2]

This necessity for understanding is another way of stating the necessity of developing empathy between counselor and counselee—empathy which comes best when we tap the source springs of *agape* love by focusing upon the love of God in Jesus Christ. The relationship between empathy and sympathy is clarified in the following definition of empathy:

> Apprehension of the state of mind of another person without feeling (as in sympathy) what the other feels. While the empathetic process is primarily intellectual, emotion is not precluded, but it is not the same emotion as that of the person with whom one empathizes. The parent may empathize with the child's puny rage, feeling pity or amusement, whereas in sympathy he would feel rage along with the child. The attitude in empathy is one of acceptance and understanding, of an implicit "I see how you feel."[3]

The word "understanding" is the key thought in empathy. It is primarily an intellectual perception but includes also a sensitivity to the feelings of the counselee.

[2] Clinebell, p. 63.
[3] Horace B. and Ava Champney English, *A Comprehensive Dictionary of Psychological and Psychoanalytical Terms* (New York: McKay, 1958).

In the New Testament a number of different Greek words are translated "understanding," "mind," "heart." Each of these Greek words sheds light on the nature of empathy.

The word *dianoia* is translated "understanding" in Ephesians 1:18 (KJV) and 4:18 and in I John 5:20. The prefix *dia* means "through; channel (of an act); by means of." *Noia* comes from *nous,* which means mind, particularly the mind in thought, or attitude, feeling. The whole word may be summarized as "deep thought," "understanding," "intelligence," "meaning." The implication is that understanding and meaning are gained only by hard and deep thinking. For the counselor this means that he will achieve an understanding of the counselee when he thinks and feels through his thoughts and feelings.

The word *psuchē* is the Greek word for soul, the animating principle of life. It is also translated "heart" and "mind" in a few places. It comes from the root *psuchō* which originally meant "to breathe"—voluntarily but gently, in contrast to hard blowing, or an inanimate breeze. I like to apply this interesting early meaning to empathy. The relationship of the counselor and the counselee is a voluntary one; the counselor's concern must be like a gentle breathing to catch some faint fragrance which otherwise might go unnoticed. Every counselor must have this sensitive, animate ability—a sensitivity of thought and of feeling to discover the meaning which the counselee is trying to convey. This indeed is empathy.

Still another word for understanding is *sunesis,* which is a mental putting together. This is an act of the intellect or reason that puts separate pieces together to make a whole, rather like fitting the pieces of a jigsaw puzzle together to make a complete picture. This word is used in Colossians 1:9 and 2:2. In II Timothy, 2:7 the word is used in a prayer that the Lord would give Timothy understanding in all things. What a fitting prayer for a young pastor! What could be more important or valuable than this kind of understanding for a minister as a servant of Christ concerned with meeting the needs of his parishioners?

And the fact that understanding or empathy is important enough to be made the object of prayer means that the writer of the epistle believed that God would give this understanding to His servant.

Colossians 1:9 is also a prayer for understanding. Here Paul prays that the Colossians may have a "spiritual understanding"—in other words, that understanding have a supernatural quality. Such understanding or empathy is appropriate for the regenerated person, the religious or Christian person. "Spiritual understanding" is of a high quality both in importance and origin, for it is indeed closely related to the understanding God has of His children everywhere.

All of these words—including the one found in I Corinthians 14:20 (*phrēn*)—show us that understanding requires intelligence. If we want this kind of understanding as pastoral counselors, we need to study hard for greater ability to put things together intelligently. The result will be a deeper understanding and empathy with our counselees.

The root from which the noun *sunesis* is taken is the verb *suniēmi* (used in I Tim. 1:7). It also means "to put together mentally," and in addition means "to comprehend, consider, gain insight." It carries with it something of a charge to be wise.

When the young King Solomon was given a chance to choose the gift he most desired from God, he chose wisdom— that is, knowledge with understanding. Later he charged the young men to whom he wrote in the book of Proverbs, to "get wisdom and with all thy getting, get understanding" (Prov. 4:7, KJV).

Incidentally, a careful examination of the book of Proverbs would prove a rewarding study. Look up the word "understanding" in a comprehensive concordance and study the passages in which this word is used. Proverbs stresses the countless uses of understanding in our relationships to our fellow men.

Developing understanding requires concentration and effort on the part of a counselor, what the Greeks called *noeō,* "to exercise the mind, observe; to comprehend, consider, think"—

that is to understand. An aid to the development of this under-standing is the thoughtful study and observation of the visible things which God has created and placed around us. This study of the visible creation can increase our understanding of the invisible things with which we must deal in our counseling relationship.

Being sense-organ-bound as we are, we must make use of the senses in order to understand and empathize. The skillful pastoral counselor observes very carefully not only the words which the counselee speaks but also the inflection of his voice, his non-verbal communication such as posture, gesture, facial expression and other indications of emotion. A part of learning to be empathetic, therefore, is observing every aspect of the counselee's attempt to communicate to us, both verbal and non-verbal.

As we gather factual information from our biographical study of the counselee and begin to put together the various impressions and perceptions we have gained through contact with him, we become increasingly empathetic and capable of being helpful in our counselor-counselee relationship. We learn to look for and catch his significant words or actions. This is a life-time study, but it is well worth the time and effort, for only so can we get beyond the surface contacts and impressions and see the depths of the soul and the yearnings, longings, and needs that are unmet in the counselee.

The book *Non-Verbal Communication: Notes on the Visual Perception of Human Relations* by Jurgen Ruesch and Weldon Kees is very helpful in this area.[4] It is made up largely of photographs illustrative of the various ways in which we receive messages from other people. Many of the more obvious contacts and experiences we take for granted, and therefore, seldom associate with the message which comes to us through these various avenues of communication. Non-verbal messages may

[4] Berkeley: University of California Press, 1956.

be meaningful and clear to the sender whereas the receiver because of blocks or blindnesses within himself may fail to catch their significance.

And the reverse may also be true. The receiver may pick up clues as to what is being sent non-verbally, though the sender may have blocks that keep him from knowing that he is sending anything. Sometimes these messages may be coming from a deeper level which is very meaningful, though this may not be apparent to the sender on the conscious level.

It is at this point that we need to become more sensitive to the deeper meanings of life's messages as they come to us every hour of our waking existence. The more anxious and needy a counselee is, the more likely he is to send a variety of these non-verbal messages to us. The authors use the word "empathetic-symbolic" under which terms they classify all the various types of communication with which we are familiar.

Ruesch and Kees also discuss what they call "empathetic assessment" (pp. 57ff.). They point out that "from knowledge of an experience with his own body, one person is capable of inferring another's sensations or judging the condition of the latter's organism. Sometimes movements carried out by particular muscular groups or pointing toward special body areas stand out with arresting significance." In the pages which follow there are numerous photographs illustrating such empathetic significance as "total appearance leads to initial distinctions"; "what children's faces can express"; "body detail can be informative"; "habit patterns"; "when posture reflects moods and attitudes"; "when intra-personal gesture becomes interpersonally informative."

Because of this human characteristic of communicating on a non-verbal level, it is vitally important that the counselor be genuine and honest with himself. Phoniness is very apparent and is far more damaging than is sometimes realized by counselors and ministers. It is very true that "as a man thinketh in his heart, so is he," for "out of the heart are the issues of life."

4. ENCOURAGING
CATHARSIS

⨉〰〰〰〰〰〰〰〰〰〰〰〰〰〰〰〰〰〰〰〰〰〰〰〰〰〰〰〰⨉

A fifteen-year-old girl sat in my office with a sad and serious expression on her face. She opened the conversation by saying, "I don't understand about God. What's He like, anyway?"

Knowing nothing about her family background, I replied, "Oh, He's like a father!"

Immediately the whole atmosphere changed. Her face suddenly showed signs of fear mixed with strong anger as she gripped the arms of her chair. Then clinching her fists and pounding them together, she shouted, "Oh, no—not like that!" Then she broke into loud sobs.

In the remainder of the hour she poured out the story of a drunken brute who was her father. He never came home sober. The first sight of him approaching sent fear and anger through the entire family. The moment he entered the house they knew they could expect only cursing, vulgarity, and cruelty. He did not hesitate to beat anyone who crossed his path with whatever was available. There was no love, no sympathy, no control.

Only pain and anxiety accompanied his presence in the home.

When she had finished pouring out her story, she wiped her eyes and said, "Thank you! I feel much better now!"

This experience was a "catharsis"—a pouring out of deep feeling she had held locked up inside for years because she had never before dared to express them to an adult.

The Bible records many instances where the Holy Spirit as the Wonderful Counselor demonstrates some of the basic principles that have more recently been discovered and identified in the field of pastoral counseling. For example, it is quite evident throughout the Old and New Testaments that God always finds access to the individual through establishing a relationship of empathy with him. Again and again the Spirit of God, speaking either through the prophets or directly to the heart, begins where the person *is* and demonstrates His understanding and concern for that person. Empathy is established in a variety of ways to meet the variety of needs, moods, thoughts, and feelings of each individual.

The Bible also describes a number of cathartic experiences, such as happens when one is overtaken by a crisis and stands helpless in the presence of God. This was Isaiah's experience in the temple after the death of his friend, King Uzziah; God spoke to him through the vision of the seraphim and of His own presence filling the temple. In the presence of such holiness, Isaiah was made acutely aware of his sinfulness and was moved to confess it to God.[1]

Another instance of catharsis involved King David after his adultery with Bathsheba and his murder of Uriah, Bathsheba's husband.[2] Here the agent of catharsis was the prophet Nathan. By a parable Nathan brought David's sin clearly to mind. "You are the man," Nathan said, after confronting David with the reality of his sin after David had by his reaction to the parable

[1] Isaiah 6:1–5.
[2] II Samuel 12:1–15.

condemned himself. Then he proceeded to speak for God, tell-ing David of the punishment which would come upon him as a result of his sin. David's response was, "I have sinned against the Lord"—a genuine cathartic experience. And because it was sincere and a genuine repentance rather than mere remorse, the prophet told him, "The Lord also has put away your sins; you shall not die."

There are also many examples in the New Testament of persons whom the Holy Spirit brought to the cathartic stage in their relationship with Him. An outstanding example is Simon Peter. After declaring that he would die with Christ rather than deny Him, Peter proceeded to deny Him three times in one night as the Master had predicted.

Later that evening Peter stood in the high priest's courtyard watching Jesus' trial from a distance. At one point Jesus looked at Peter—a look that touched his heart and brought him to his senses. He went out and wept bitterly. Peter's catharsis took the form of release of emotion through weeping. This step was a vital one in the process of the Master's dealings with Peter. Until a person comes face to face with his wrongdoing and confesses his need for help, it is impossible for him to change or to benefit from help.

The cathartic experience constitutes both a tremendous re-sponsibility and an access to infinite resources for the pastoral counselor. Because of the value of catharsis, he will at times have to use the confrontation approach[3] to bring the counselee to it. But more often his empathetic listening and love will lead the counselee to trust him and to pour out his deeper anxiety and concerns.

Romans 2:4 expresses the dynamics of the counselor-counselee relationship in an atmosphere of *agape* love. "Or despisest thou the riches of his goodness and forbearance and longsuffering; not knowing that the goodness of God leadeth

[3] See chapter 5.

thee to repentance?" (KJV). When true empathy exists, as described in the previous chapter, the way is cleared for the counselee, because he feels secure, to pour out his anxieties, fears, hostilities, concerns. He knows that in spite of his failures and sinfulness the counselor will accept him in love and, as God does, will give assurance of that acceptance. Actually what he is needing and seeking is acceptance in the form of forgiveness. The pastoral counselor should be an expert in his knowledge of God's love and forgiveness through Christ and be able to communicate this to his counselee in the empathetic atmosphere and relationship.

In the next verses of Romans 2 (5, 6, KJV), we are told the effects of refusal to give in to catharsis in counseling. "But after thy hardness and impenitent heart treasurest up unto thyself wrath against the day of wrath and revelation of the righteous judgment of God; who will render to every man according to his deeds." Then the way in which God will deal with these is spelled out in the following verses which we need not discuss at this point.

From the psychological and psychiatric standpoint, to refuse to give expression to the deeper feelings such as remorse, penitence, bitterness, hostility, fear, and others may result in what the psychiatrist calls "repression." Repression means that a continuing refusal to face the facts and admit them may actually result in "forgetting" them by repressing them into the unconscious part of the mind. The results are well known in the psychiatric profession, and the fruits are not good. Repression merely delays the expression of the hostility or fear and diverts it from a normal and natural form of release to an abnormal and unnatural form which brings on physical or mental and emotional illness. The pastoral counselor needs to be aware of this danger, and therefore to make time and opportunity as well as to provide atmosphere for genuine catharsis.

It hardly seems necessary to warn counselors of the dangers of adopting a judgmental attitude toward counselees. A judgmental attitude on the part of the pastoral counselor will devastate the relationship and completely remove any possibility of catharsis. When a person gets the courage to confess his own faults only to find that he is condemned and reproved and threatened by the counselor, he withdraws from the relationship. He becomes the victim of a deeper-seated guilt, and his mental, emotional, and spiritual condition is worsened rather than relieved or healed.

When God spoke to David through Nathan the prophet, he did not leave David in a state of utter hopelessness and despair. He did honestly state to him some of the inevitable effects and results of his sin, but along with this he hastened to give assurance of God's forgiveness and love. When David acknowledged his sin, Nathan, who was acting in the role of counselor, said: "The Lord also has put away your sin; you shall not die. Nevertheless, because by this deed you have utterly scorned the Lord, the child that is born to you shall die."

Nathan's response shows us an important factor in counseling. When catharsis has taken place, a counselor is not justified either in leaving the counselee without hope or in giving him false hope that through catharsis all the damage done to his own personality or to others will be completely healed. Of course the good counselor, with confidence in the presence and power of the Holy Spirit, never doubts that in God's own time and way complete healing can and will take place. But to say that this is to come without suffering or pain would be to mislead the counselee. We can no more defy the laws of God in interpersonal relationships than we can defy the laws of nature and survive. Fortunately, our God is not only *just* but also *merciful,* and the pastoral counselor knows this and is under obligation to communicate this vital factor to his counselee at the proper time and in the proper way.

The book of Job gives us an interesting study in catharsis. Here we are given insight into the inner workings of the mind and heart of Job. Suffering and pain had come into his life, and crisis after crisis had brought him to the point of desperation. His so-called "friends" came to "counsel" him, but about all they accomplished was to lead him to search himself, his motives, his attitudes, and his actions more critically. Their judgmental attitudes were not helpful but rather added to his depression and desperation.

But in the end Job stood in the presence of God. As he listened to the Holy Spirit who seemed to ask question after question which searched his soul, Job repented in "dust and ashes."

> Then Job answered the Lord:
> "I know that thou canst do all things,
>   and that no purpose of thine can be thwarted.
> 'Who is this that hides counsel without knowledge?'
> Therefore I have uttered what I did not understand,
>   things too wonderful for me, which I did not know.
>
> 'Hear, and I will speak;
>   I will question you, and you declare to me,'
> I had heard of thee by the hearing of the ear,
>   but now my eye sees thee;
> therefore I despise myself,
>   and repent in dust and ashes."
>
> —JOB 42:1–6

Catharsis was the necessary step at this point in Job's life and relationship to his Lord. The relief and joy which followed, as recorded in verses 10–17, are illustrative of the peace and joy and rewards which come to the person who has undergone catharsis and received acceptance from his counselor and forgiveness from God.

How does the counselor encourage emotional release? Dr. Clinebell answers that question as follows:

By listening and responding to feelings. More specifically, the following approaches tend to facilitate catharsis:
    (1) Avoid asking informational questions beyond the mini-

mum needed to obtain essential factual data. Informational questions tend to pull the person away from feelings.

(2) Ask about feelings—e.g., "How did you feel when the chairman ignored you?"

(3) Respond to feelings rather than intellectual content. Reflect feelings, using feeling words in doing so. "You really felt clobbered by what happened!" "This hurts down deep!" "Let's see if I catch what you're feeling here."

(4) Watch for doors which lead to the feeling level of communication. These include feeling words, emotion in the voice or face, protesting too much, self-contradictions (indicating inner conflicts), and discussion of parental or other crucial need-satisfying relationships. Responding to these often leads to deeper levels of feelings.

(5) Be especially alert for negative feelings. These are the most frequently repressed and the most in need of being brought into the psychological sunlight of a therapeutic relationship.

(6) Avoid both premature interpretations of why people function or feel certain ways and premature advice. Both of these are tempting traps since they offer the counselor ways of feeling useful, intelligent, in control, and thus less anxious. Both interpretations and advice tend to block the flow of feelings (p. 70).

The pastoral counselor's role in providing the opportunity for catharsis is to show active concern and to listen to the counselee as he unburdens his soul. Any indication of a lack of interest, any expression of disapproval or of a judgmental attitude will only do harm at this point. Catharsis takes place only when the counselee feels secure enough to bare himself before another. If the pastoral counselor by his facial expression, tone of voice, or words, gives the slightest indication that he is not an understanding, sympathetic counselor, then catharsis is hindered.

We cannot overlook the significance and necessity of the work of the Holy Spirit in preparing the counselee and enabling him to unburden his soul in the presence of another. We know that a part of the work of the Holy Spirit is that of pointing out or "convicting" the counselee of his sins, and only when this takes place is the counselee ready for catharsis. Of course, the counselor provides some help in preparation, and to that extent he becomes an agent of the Holy Spirit in performing this cathartic function. The counselor, while listening and giving acceptance, enables the counselee to look back into his life and lift the blinds of his soul so that the sunlight of another's acceptance may enter into the dark corners where guilt has been residing for so long.

There are a number of specific things which lead to catharsis or assist it in the counseling relationship. I remember one counselee who was terribly disturbed because of her husband's seeming loss of love. He had turned away to another woman. Connie came in for counseling. She found it difficult to respond to the suggestion that she fill out a battery of inventories to enable both of us to understand the nature and variety of her inmost feelings. Eventually, however, she agreed to it. Instead of spending the usual amount of time on these inventories, she spent most of the morning and then went on through the lunch hour trying to respond to the various statements.

The following morning Connie called me. "Could I see you a little while this morning after I come from the doctor's office? I feel I need to talk with you."

When she was seated in my office, she began, "In filling out those inventories yesterday I saw myself as four people. I really don't know who I am, and I feel I must find out. Actually, I realize now that I haven't been able to know or be myself for years. Perhaps this is the reason for the breakdown of our marriage."

She now realized, she continued, that years ago she had rejected her husband because he seemed to desire to have intercourse in what she thought to be an abnormal way. Ever since then she felt the gap had been growing between them. Having worked with the husband, I was able to check her insight against his expression of feeling and found it to be accurate. I reassured Connie and immediately I could see the expression of her face change to great relief. She had gained a degree of understanding of what she had done to her husband and to their marriage.

The fact that for the first time in her life she was able to talk about this deep-seated resentment and feeling of guilt gave Connie tremendous relief. She was now ready for the first time to talk with me about ways and means by which she might discover herself and through doing so reveal herself to her husband. Here I feel the Holy Spirit used the experience of filling out inventories to prepare Connie for the catharsis which she so badly needed.

I have known many cases where the use of confrontation has brought about catharsis. A series of interviews over a considerable length of time had failed to break through to Dave. Aware of the need for catharsis, I was giving much time, thought, and prayer in search of ways and means to bring this about.

Finally in a certain interview, it seemed clear to me that Dave needed to be confronted boldly with the real problem which I had seen but which he had never been able to admit. "Aren't you trying to tell me that you are afraid that you are a homosexual?" I asked. The result was amazing. Immediately Dave broke down and sobbed for quite a while.

"Yes, yes, how did you know?" he said finally.

Then, before I could respond, he said, "Of course you know. I was doing everything in my power to tell you without actually admitting it in words to you or anyone else. Knowing this, can you still accept me as a counselee and friend?"

Having built a strong rapport with Dave in preceding interviews, I had no difficulty in convincing him that he was fully accepted and understood and would not be rejected as he so greatly feared. The relief was evident and almost miraculous in its result.

From that time on we were able to begin the work of restoring Dave's defeated and deflated ego to the point where once more he could accept himself as a human being worthy of the society in which he lived.

When we know the truth, the truth does "set us free." I believe that this is definitely the work of the Holy Spirit within the heart of both counselor and counselee. The acceptance the counselor is able to give under such circumstances is a direct effect of the Holy Spirit's work in his mind and heart, enabling him to see beyond the deeds to the person, and to understand something of the depth of the stress and strain which led him to such conduct and behavior.

5. USING CONFRONTATION

~~~~~~

At ten P.M. *my phone rang. The woman's anxious voice was* appealing for her husband. Would I meet them at my office as soon as possible? I knew the couple quite well through months of appointments made, then often broken just when there was a possibility of the dentist-husband making some progress.

"Just one question," I said. "Will your husband face up to his personal responsibility, or will he back off when he is confronted with it?"

After a pause, during which she relayed this question to her husband, she said, "He promises he will cooperate fully . . . he's desperate!"

At ten-thirty we were helping steady him as he half staggered to the office from the parking lot.

Three years of psychoanalysis had provided him with countless alibis for his conduct. Not once had this man admitted or accepted personal responsibility for his irresponsible behavior.

But that night, confronted by the results of his irresponsibility, he finally did.

At the close of the last chapter I mentioned confrontation in connection with catharsis. Confrontation is so effective in certain conditions that I feel justified in giving an entire chapter to its consideration.

In II Samuel 11 and 12, we have the account of David's great sin against Uriah and his wife Bathsheba to which I have referred previously. Now, however, I wish to stress the method used by Nathan in dealing with David and his need.

Nathan used a parable to prepare the way for confronting David with his sin.

> "There were two men in a certain city [Nathan said], the one rich and the other poor. The rich man had very many flocks and herds; but the poor man had nothing but one little ewe lamb, which he had bought. And he brought it up, and it grew up with him and with his children; it used to eat of his morsel, and drink from his cup, and lie in his bosom, and it was like a daughter to him. Now there came a traveler to the rich man, and he was unwilling to take one of his own flock or herd to prepare for the wayfarer who had come to him, but he took the poor man's lamb, and prepared it for the man who had come to him." Then David's anger was greatly kindled against the man; and he said to Nathan, "As the Lord lives, the man who has done this deserves to die; and he shall restore the lamb fourfold, because he did this thing, and because he had no pity."
>
> Nathan said to David, "You are the man. Thus says the Lord, the God of Israel, I anointed you king over Israel, and I delivered you out of the hand of Saul; and I gave you your master's house, and your master's wives into your bosom, and gave you the house of Israel and of Judah; and if this were too little, I would add to you as much more. Why have you despised the word of the Lord, to do what is evil in his sight? You have smitten Uriah the Hittite with the sword, and have taken his wife to be your wife,

and have slain him with the sword of the Ammonites. Now therefore the sword shall never depart from your house, because you have despised me, and have taken the wife of Uriah the Hittite to be your wife."

Then Nathan went on to deliver the remainder of God's message to the guilt-stricken David, confronting him with the totality and seriousness of his sin. David's response was to admit his sin openly: "I have sinned against the Lord." "The Lord has also put away your sin," Nathan told him; "you shall not die. Nevertheless, because by this deed you have utterly scorned the Lord, the child that is born to you shall die."[1]

This was indeed a dramatic and traumatic experience for David. But it was necessary. Because of the depth and nature of the wrong he had done to Uriah, to his office as king of Israel, to Uriah's wife, and to the unborn child, David had to be confronted with the total picture.

It is important, however, to notice that the judgment placed upon David for his sin was not without an expression of the love and mercy of God in providing pardon and forgiveness. When Nathan was able to say, "The Lord has also put away your sin; you shall not die," he was giving reassurance to David of his acceptance by God and his pardon as a result of his true repentance. Had David not been confronted by Nathan in this way it is doubtful that he would have come to recognize or admit the fact of his sinfulness and need for forgiveness.

A favorable discussion of this incident may seem very frightening and out of place in a book on counseling, especially against the background of emphasis on the client-centered approach which has been so commonly used by ministers in their pastoral counseling. To act like Nathan would seemingly make the pastor step out of his role as counselor and project himself into the role of a prophet who stands behind the pulpit judging

[1] II Samuel 12:1–15.

his congregation. This, of course, is the danger if this approach is not wisely and carefully used.

On the other hand, it is now well known and understood that Protestant pastoral counselors have tended not to take guilt as seriously as the destructive effects warrant. They have too often avoided the use of confrontation. As a result, they have at times been guilty of "cruel kindness" as Clinebell calls it (p. 226).

Unfortunately, it is true that people do not change until they experience actual pain or suffering in their present situation. When the situation is a result of wrongdoing, then anything less than frank and firm confrontation will be both useless and even hurtful in the ministry of healing.

But before dealing in more detail with this approach, I would like to emphasize strongly some of the dangers which may accompany it unless it is properly used.

First of all, as we have already noted, there is the real danger that the counselor may, in the eyes of the counselee, become a "judge." If the troubled person ever begins to feel this way, his guilt feelings will increase and it will be extremely hard for him to find forgiveness and reconciliation. When one is seriously enough disturbed by his longstanding guilt to be deeply depressed and to seek aid from a counselor, he is in no condition to be confronted suddenly or indiscriminately by his counselor.

A judging confrontation, unprepared for, may end any relationship which would make counseling possible. The person already feels guilty and ashamed, and to be judged and condemned rather than understood and accepted is nothing less than absolute rejection. A person laden with guilt already feels cut off and rejected by all that stands for rightness and justice; he surely does not need to be condemned more by the one to whom he goes seeking help.

The pastor also needs to remember that he is not commissioned to sit in judgment on anyone. Christ himself made it very clear that His followers are not to judge, lest they themselves be judged. He assures us that judgment belongs to God, and that

He will mete out justice along with mercy according to His all-wise will.

Many people seek help from their pastors because they do feel guilty and are longing for restoration with God and His people. If the human person who represents God turns his back upon the "sinner," he is misrepresenting God and is actually placing himself above God. He is doing what God himself would not do—rejecting the penitent sinner. There is abundant evidence of God's acceptance in both the Old and the New Testaments. Every pastor needs to remind himself again and again that he has no right ever to sit in judgment upon his fellow man.

It is as true now as it was in the day it was written that "all we like sheep have gone astray; we have turned every one to his own way." Because we are all guilty in God's sight, He has made a way for us to be pardoned and healed through the sacrifice of His own son on Calvary. It is, therefore, because of what Christ did for us that we may stand before God's judgment while assured of pardon, forgiveness, and restoration in God's family, no matter how grave our sin may have been.

Another word here is more by way of a reminder than warning. The pastor, if he is true to his title (which means, of course, "shepherd"), is concerned with the healing, not the condemning or punishing, of his sheep. He has a heart of compassion and understanding as well as great sympathy. The least the pastor can do, and the most he can do, is to express his Christlike love through genuine acceptance of the counselee with all of his sinfulness and weakness, just as though he were a bruised or injured sheep. He will draw him close to his heart and provide him with assurance of the pardon which is available through Christ from the Father.

The nature of a pastor's preaching ministry and the image he has in the community are important prerequisites to the use of the confrontational approach in counseling. If his reputation is that of a condemning, angry judge who hurls his anathemas at his wounded and sinful people, who will dare approach him for help? And who could receive help by the use of confrontation in counseling?

In other words, before a pastor uses the confrontational approach he needs to be sure that his own attitude is one of compassion, understanding, and acceptance rather than of judgment and rejection.

Once one has this attitude he is in a position to think of using the confrontational approach in counseling. Until then, however, there may be real danger and too great a risk in resorting to this method. One example should illustrate the importance of this fact.

A stranger once entered my office seeking counseling. He was a man in his middle forties, and his face showed lines of suffering, anxiety, and fear. I received him not knowing what his problem was, but when he told me about it, I realized that there was so much in it that was wrong and hurtful to himself and to others that a judgmental attitude might have seemed appropriate from me as a pastor.

I was aware, however, of the danger of making such a person feel rejected, so I gave him complete acceptance. After some months of weekly interviews he told me that he had gone to five different ministers seeking help. Each time he had found them standing in judgment over him. His sense of guilt had increased and he had not found any relief. He had come to me as the last resort with the definite intent of making no further efforts. If this try failed, he had made up his mind that he could not live any longer under this cloud. If I treated him as other ministers had done, he was going to take his life that very day.

How fortunate that the Holy Spirit guided me in my attitude toward him! Had I done other than accept him, would I not have been party to the complete destruction of a life, leaving a widow and two children without support?

Having issued this warning, let us move on to the value and purpose of confrontational counseling and the Holy Spirit's relationship to the counselor and counselee. The ultimate purpose of the confrontational approach in counseling is to bring the person to an awareness of his need and a determination to do all within his power, under the guidance of a counselor, to correct the wrongs he has done and to be strong in resisting the temptation in the future.

The counselor's theme in this approach should always be that of "speaking the truth in love." If love is not present and genuine, this approach can have deadly effects. Certainly the counselee needs and wants the truth, but he must have it in a form which he can accept. This is in the atmosphere of genuine love and acceptance on the part of the counselor. He definitely needs to "repent" of the wrongs he has done, but also he must be able to realize the presence of the Holy Spirit as the regenerating and cleansing agent of a forgiving God.

We must, therefore, stress that the basic essential for effective confrontation is the counselor's acceptance. If this attitude is communicated to the counselee, and a strong empathy is established, then the relationship will not be broken when the moment of confrontation arrives but will rather be strengthened.

Only when empathy is established is the climate ready for confrontation; until then it is neither wise nor helpful. The tone of voice, the mood of the counselee and counselor, and the genuineness of the relationship will have prepared the counselee for the shock of confrontation.

Many pastors avoid the use of this approach under any circumstances for fear that the relationship will be broken. But this is a weakness in their counseling. I hope I have sufficiently emphasized the preliminary steps which, if properly taken, will deepen and strengthen the relationship rather than breaking it, and bring about results which probably could never have been accomplished otherwise. The counselor "who is always accepting and permissive, and never acceptingly confronting, is unwittingly guilty of 'cruel kindness.' "[2]

[2] Clinebell, p. 226.

At this point we need to inject a principle which, until fairly recent years, was either not known or was rejected by the familiar pastoral counseling approach. Paul Tillich calls it "the principle of mutuality."

> The basic principle for the attitude of pastoral counseling is mutuality. The counselor must participate in the situation of the person needing care. This participation expresses itself not only in words of acceptance, but also in ways of communicating to the counselee the fact that the counselor was and is in the same situation. This can be done by telling a concrete story in which the counselor experienced the same negativities for which the counselee needs care. It can be in words which make it clear to the counselee that the counselor understands well on the basis of his own experience. If such a thing happens, the subject-object situation—the great danger for all pastoral care—is overcome.[3]

This is a depth of relating to the counselee which many counselors fear and have actually been instructed not to use. Of course it must only be used at the proper time and in the proper way. It should never be imposed upon the counselee to the point that the counselor's problems become the focus of attention.

But for the counselee to know that the counselor has experienced similar distress removes the counselor from the pedestal upon which many pastors have been placed by our society. This effort to meet the troubled person on the "home grounds" of his experience sometimes is the best possible preparation for the use of confrontation in counseling.

A statement is attributed to John Bunyan which is applicable here. When he saw an alcoholic staggering along the road he said, "There but for the grace of God go I." It is the introduction and recognition of this "grace" which is the saving factor in the counselee's experience. It provides hope and assurance to the troubled person to know that the counselor will do what he can to bring the counselee into the awareness and acceptance of that grace.

[3] Clinebell, p. 230.

Here we must recognize the active presence and work of the Holy Spirit both in the counselor and the counselee. When the fact of grace and forgiveness is revealed to the counselee, we know that the Holy Spirit must be working in his heart to open the eyes and ears of his soul to receive it. And unless there is this inner work of the Spirit, the words may fall like seed on stony ground and be lost.

Various means are available in the confrontational counseling process. One is the use of a tape recording of an interview, which, of course, can only be made with the permission of the people involved. Recording a couple's interaction in the presence of the counselor, for instance, can help both husband and wife recognize their individual responsibility and guilt. Hearing their discussion may bring insight and the realization of what is happening to them, especially when the counselor points out the significance.

Another effective method is to discuss with the counselee the destructive consequences of his irresponsible conduct and its effect upon the lives of those whom he intimately touches—his wife, children, parents, and others.

The method which Nathan the prophet used with David might on occasion be useful—an analogy or parable which includes the basic elements of the counselee's situation. Sometimes the use of another person's similar experience may take the heat off of the counselee sufficiently for him to listen to and accept the similarity of that situation to his own.

A prayerful concern on the part of the counselor is necessary and valuable at all times, but particularly so before using the confrontational approach. By this I do not mean that the counselor will pause in the midst of an interview and say, "Let us pray," or that he will resort to prayer in some conspicuous manner in the presence of the counselee. I believe a counselor can be in a prayerful mood while he looks straight into the eyes of the person before him. He does not need to close his eyes at all—that might frighten the counselee rather than maintain or strengthen empathy. I have found myself on many occasions praying what Dr. Frank Laubach calls a "flash prayer" (perhaps not even a complete sentence) to the Holy Spirit, the "Counselor." It is often amazing what calm and confidence result in the relationship.

Here I speak from personal experience and not from theory. On many occasions, when I was convinced that a confrontation was necessary to break through the crust that the counselee wore, but was very uncertain as to the best moment at which to introduce the confrontation, I have silently and unobtrusively asked the Holy Spirit, "Is this the time? If not, when?"

Even then, at times, I have been so uncertain and fearful that harm might result that I have added (at least in thought), "Please don't let me make a mistake either in waiting too long or in moving too fast."

There are those who properly fear a misuse of the reliance upon the Holy Spirit—by demanding too much of "the effectiveness of prayer" and neglecting the use of all knowledge, reason, and common sense. I firmly believe that all the knowledge we may gain is essential. It is not a question of either/or but of both/and. We must use the best possible knowledge and tools available, but must also have a childlike reliance upon the presence, wisdom, and willingness of the Holy Spirit to guide the counseling process. In matters so vitally important and far-reaching as the human lives that come for counseling, one should hardly be so foolhardy as to run unnecessary risks by relying merely upon the limitations of human knowledge.

Forty years in the ministry, much of which has been given to pastoral counseling, have convinced me that all the knowledge we may have of counseling techniques, processes, etc. is inadequate in some cases. A failure to realize one's need for divine guidance may result in worse than failure. I stress this here because no type of counseling can be either more dangerous or more precipitous in bringing about constructive results than the confrontational approach. Yet with all its dangers and risks it still may be necessary to use it with certain counselees. A counselor would seem quite foolish, if not egotistical, to assume that he understood the counselee so well that he could take such risks without the guidance of One with superior understanding of the thoughts and intents of the hearts of men.

It is both presumptuous and unnecessary, I feel, for any pastor to assume that prayer for the guidance of the Holy Spirit and a prayerful mood and attitude in all these relationships is merely superficial or pietistic. I have found it to be most real and essential. To the extent that my efforts in the counseling ministry have been effective and lasting, I attribute these results to this kind of person-to-person relationship between the counselor and the Holy Spirit.

Returning from this parenthesis to ways and means of confronting individuals in counseling, the method used by Alcoholics Anonymous is at times effective and useful. This requires the counselee to make "a searching and fearless moral inventory." In this inventory he must admit to God, himself, and another human being the exact nature of the wrongs resulting from his failure—in the case of AA, his drinking. Also, it is helpful to suggest that the counselee make a list of all those persons whom he may have harmed, and include ways and means by which he might make amends to these persons whenever possible. There are times, of course, when it is impossible to make amends without injuring someone else, and one should naturally avoid hurting others.

The next step in counseling, following the actual confrontation, must be to lead the person to confess his wrongs to the counselor—his fellow man—and to God. Writing them out sometimes helps a person to be more definitive, and such precise statements may strengthen his motivation to seek forgiveness and to experience the relief that comes only through forgiveness.

After confession, it is part of the pastoral counselor's priestly function and responsibility to make a statement of absolution.

Such a statement has little value, however, apart from the counselor's genuine knowledge and assurance of the readiness and willingness of God to forgive.

The pastoral counselor, in the minds of most counselees, stands as God's representative on earth; because of his training and personal experience, he is qualified to speak "for God" because he knows God's mind in such matters. Here of course there is abundant Scripture to support the counselor. "If we confess our sins, he is faithful and just, and will forgive our sins and cleanse us from all unrighteousness" (I John 1:9). Psalm 103:12 is another: "As far as the east is from the west, so far does he remove our transgressions from us." Another is Luke 7:48.

But the work of the counselor is not finished at this point. Although a person has become aware of his sins and wrong-doings through confrontation, has confessed them, and has heard them declared forgiven through the counselor's statement of absolution, the counselee must still be led to do more. The next step must be *restitution*. If there is any possible way he can make amends for the harm he has done others, or can return that which he has unjustly taken from others, he should be encouraged to do so. Restitution involves action; words and faith without action are usually useless or meaningless.

It is often necessary for the counselor to help the counselee take the necessary steps to bring about *reconciliation* to those whom he has wronged or he feels have wronged him. Reconciliation with our fellow men is basic and must come before our reconciliation with God. This fact should not be disregarded by the counselor.

The pastor counselor should never be hesitant or timid in his counseling about what he regards as right. However, he does need to ask himself at every point—and find a satisfactory answer—"Why and how is this thing right or wrong?" If he is reasonably aware that this sense of right and wrong is not based upon some selfish, moralistic, or self-righteous concept, but has a deeper basis on man's relationship to man and to God, then he has no reason to hesitate in taking a stand upon this position.

The counselor's conviction as to the rightness of behavior must never take the form of passing judgment upon those who differ with him or are "guilty" of a different behavior. God has demanded that the matter of judgment rest in His hands and not be tampered with by human beings. If the pastor is immature emotionally and has not been able to resolve his own hostilities and resentments, it may be difficult for him to use the confrontational approach wisely or effectively. His need to be "judged" will unconsciously lead him to pass judgment on others and hence cancel out the possible values of this approach.

6. PROVIDING
INSPIRATION

‹‹

Raymond Zigler was about as sad and dejected a man as I had ever seen in my counseling office. His life story easily accounted for his forlorn expression. Added to his sadness was bitterness and hostility to a degree that isolated him more and more from those he touched. But a friend of mine had referred him to me for help, and help him I must. So I began to listen with close attention both to his words and to his silences.

Raymond was born out of wedlock. His childhood was devoid of love and security. His adolescence was best described by the word delinquent. He was forever in trouble. With no real parents who loved or wanted or cared for him; with teachers who seemed more bent on scolding, punishing, and blaming than on helping; with a record of arrests and punishment; with repeated failure in his attempts to secure work or keep a job once obtained, Raymond saw no purpose in living. Perhaps incarceration in a penal institution offered his best chance for food, clothing and shelter! Why try any more?

What Raymond needed above everything else was inspiration; without it there was little hope of his becoming a useful member of society. To provide inspiration would not be an easy task. Yet if I really believed in the love of God for every person, and if the Holy Spirit was available to provide guidance and help, there must be a way to help Raymond.

Early interviews were largely exploratory and focused on hearing Raymond's life story. There surely must be some flicker of hope or ray of light to point the way! And there was. He knew how to set type and operate a printing press. Would he be interested in using the small, hand-operated press stored in the storeroom of the church to print the weekly bulletins for the church services?

To be made to feel wanted and useful, and to be trusted to do this job gave Raymond a new feeling. Someone actually thought he might do a useful work . . . and that within the walls of a church!

"Yes," he said "I'd like to try."

And try he did. Week after week Raymond took meticulous care and ever-increasing interest and pride in printing the bulletins. A short note was inserted in the bulletin expressing appreciation of this volunteer work done weekly by Raymond Zigler. People came to know him, and many expressed their personal appreciation of the careful work and the attractive bulletins he produced. He gradually began to accept himself as a useful person. Eventually he felt that, with the support and backing of the pastor and these people, he would get a job and make his way in the world. Inspiration had served its purpose. Raymond was employed by a printing concern through the influence of a member of the church.

Inspiration can be thought of in several ways. It implies that there is something spiritual within a person which motivates him to respond. Another idea is that one is "breathed into." When we think of the work of the Holy Spirit and the nature of spirit itself, we realize that inspiration means that which is breathed into a person—like the breath of life. Something that is truly inspiring rejuvenates, revives, motivates. So, when we speak of the counselor providing inspiration it should be clearly understood that the counselor has nothing to give unless first it is given to him.

The nature of this gift is spiritual. It is like air, or breath, or wind from God breathed into the counselor's mind and heart so that in turn he may give to others that which encourages, supports, and inspires them to greater undertakings.

I have deliberately used the word "inspiration" rather than "supportive counseling," for what I am talking about is more than merely providing support through counseling, and even more than encouragement. Actually there is no simple way to describe what I have in mind, other than to say that it is a length, depth, and breadth of counseling which goes beyond encouragement or support; it provides the counselee with new hope and with desire to change and to receive.

In this area the counselor must maintain the most intimate relationship with the Source of all wisdom, strength, courage, power—with God. This is especially true when dealing with a depressed person who has lost all hope and desire to live—there must be resources above and beyond mere human resources available to the counselor.

Words of wisdom or even of mature experience from another person are insufficient to bring a person out of a deep depression or an attitude of hopelessness and despair into the desire to live and achieve. The most a human being can do is to make suggestions, provide information and illustrations, and hope the counselee will be able to hear, accept, and therefore respond constructively to these suggestions. But I doubt seriously if this kind of person can do any of these, having seen the depth of despair and hopelessness which my counselees have reached in their lives.

Certainly this is no time for "preaching." Inspiration is not something that can be taught through the words of the counselor to the listening ear of the counselee. This is an instance where the words of Christ are appropriate—"seeing they do not see, and hearing they do not hear." They have been blinded by their disappointments and hurts until the safest haven for them seems to be their own little world. They have shut themselves off from the outside world to a large extent and are living alone within the high walls of their emotional resistances. Blocks and blind spots seem to be greater than sight or sound. Therefore the counselor may find himself shouting at the top of his voice —both literally and figuratively—to one who is totally deaf and blind to his efforts.

One might say that when a person reaches this point of impassivity, he needs to be under a psychiatrist or in an institution. No doubt this is generally true. Indeed it is entirely true when the counselee has withdrawn to the point where no one can break through his wall and receive any normal response to his approaches. If the counselee has escaped into the realm of hallucination or delusion, the counselor of course, can do little other than refer him to a more skillful and highly trained person, such as a psychiatrist. However, those of whom I am speaking here have not reached that point of withdrawal; they are hovering on the threshold between reality and unreality. They can still hear, though they are finding it increasingly difficult to respond hopefully.

The most skillful counselor with his best techniques can sometimes get through to the counselee's mind and heart and gain a response which is encouraging. But this is hardly enough to satisfy. What we need here is the divine, over and above the human touch. I believe this is available to the pastoral counselor once he has established intimate personal relationship with God and is aware of the presence and operation of the Holy Spirit.

Here we enter into that marvelous realm of the human-divine relationship which goes out beyond reason and logic, and embraces the realm of the spiritual. Mysterious and mystical as this may seem it is nonetheless real. Countless pastors and pastoral counselors, as well as other persons, have experienced the reality of this spiritual world both in centuries past and today.

A vivid illustration is found in the Book of Acts. On the day of Pentecost, the group of apostles were assembled in an upper room where they had met day by day for fellowship and prayer. They were told specifically by Christ that they would receive power after the Holy Spirit had come upon them, and they were assured also that this would take place in a few days after His resurrection and ascension.

They did not fully understand His meaning, nor did they know precisely what to expect. All they knew to do was to maintain the Christian fellowship and mutual support of their faith, and deepen and strengthen their communication with the divine resources through the channel of prayer. None of these men, as far as we know, was able to speak any language other than the common Aramaic of Palestine in that day. They had little or no knowledge of other languages either to speak or to understand them. We are told that they were very ordinary and uneducated men, fishermen, tax collectors, etc., with no college or university education. Although they were well acquainted with nature, with their jobs, with the local situation, it is doubtful if any of them had ever been inside a library or traveled outside of Palestine or the lands immediately to the north and east.

And yet, on that particular day of Pentecost, while they were meeting together in the upper room for prayer and fellowship, there came upon them the promised power. Its presence was symbolized by what is described as tongues of fire which settled on each of the people gathered there. Immediately they began to speak in other languages.

Such a gift would be called a miracle in any man's language, and a miracle indeed it was. But it seems to me that it is no more of a miracle than occurs often in the counselor—counselee relationship. In a sense the same promise made by Christ to those early apostles has been made to all those who will seek the wisdom He offers.

The apostles on the day of Pentecost needed the ability to speak in many different languages because there were people in Jerusalem from many different countries all speaking their own language. The people were amazed that these men, who were all Galileans, were able to speak in their own language so that each person could understand them. The pastoral counselor's need today usually is not for ability to speak in different foreign languages. But he does need the ability to communicate. He needs to penetrate beyond the barriers which have been thrown up for the defense of the injured ego of our counselees, to communicate with them in a form that they as individuals will be able to understand and accept.

Practically any pastor who has done any counseling can say truthfully that there are times when he has no words of wisdom to reach the counselee where he needs to be reached. So it is to his surprise and delight that he discovers sometime during the counseling session or later that the message has gotten through. He was heard, accepted, and responded to. This is a thrilling experience. Counselors often take credit, however, for being able to do a superb job of counseling when actually what happened was the direct result of the Holy Spirit working in the heart of the counselee, enabling him to hear and respond as he could not otherwise have done.

Let me give a very striking illustration of this help. I was completely frustrated in my interviews with a young couple, and felt as though the last moment of possible usefulness to them had come. There seemed to be little or no possibility of achieving anything constructive in changing their attitudes.

John, a young doctor, had come to me for marriage counseling. His wife Gloria, who was also a physician, had left him sometime before because they could not get along together. She had signed a year's contract with a hospital in another city and had no intention of returning to her husband. Since there were no children involved, it seemed possible that this marriage would end in divorce.

John made it very clear that he was not interested in religion in any shape or form; his only reason for coming was that I was qualified to do marriage counseling, and he knew no other qualified marriage counselor in the city. I assured him that I would do what I could on his terms, but inwardly I was trusting and praying silently that God would use me to reach him on deeper levels. I felt that the deterioration in his marriage must be partly due to his own lack of understanding and appreciation of his wife, or perhaps to some unwillingness or inability on his part to provide her with the necessary security and love she required.

After several interviews I suddenly felt that the time had arrived when it would be possible to enlist his wife's help toward a better adjustment. I suggested that he might call his wife long distance and see if she could or would come the following weekend.

At first John shook his head. "I am sure she won't come. She doesn't care what happens to me and has no interest in helping me."

But I wasn't convinced of this. I was compelled, as it were, to pursue the matter further, and made some additional suggestions about ways and means of enlisting her cooperation.

"Well, it won't hurt to try," John said finally.

And so we closed the interview with the understanding that if she were willing to come, he would call me. In the meantime I would keep time open on Saturday afternoon and Sunday for the interview.

In a day or two he called me. To his great surprise and amazement, Gloria had said she would fly up for this purpose.

After spending all of Saturday afternoon and a part of Sunday morning working with the couple, using every possible technique I knew to bring about some kind of communication or better understanding between them, the time was rapidly approaching when Gloria had to catch her plane back. Feeling that I had made absolutely no impression on either of them, I was utterly frustrated. Sitting behind my desk, I prayed silently that God would not let this opportunity pass by without giving some guidance or assurance that I could be helpful.

After a period of silence a compulsive thought came to me, and I found myself saying, "I wish I had two copies of some book which had short readings for each day for a month so that I could give a copy to each of you to take home. You would both read the same passage each day and jot down your reaction. By exchanging your reactions, you would discover wherein you are in agreement and wherein you differ."

The words were hardly out of my mouth before panic settled in. I had no idea what book I was speaking of, nor did I think I had two copies of *any* book on hand which I could lend, much less one that was arranged in this fashion.

In my office at this time, the bookcase was at the opposite end of the rather long room. I got up from the desk and walked very slowly toward the bookcase, still wondering what I could discover that would meet this situation.

To my utter amazement, on top of the bookcase were two new copies of David Mace's little book, *Whom God Hath Joined*. For a moment I was thrilled, but then panic set in again. The title would probably be enough to end all hope of getting the cooperation of either John or Gloria—it contained the word "God."

Then another miracle happened. I say miracle, because to this day I have not been able to recall where I read these facts. Shortly after this experience I met Dr. Mace and asked him if these facts were true. "Yes, exactly so," was his reply.

The miracle was what I said to John and Gloria about Dr. Mace. He was an internationally recognized marriage counselor from Great Britain, I told them. He had written this book from the viewpoint not of a minister but of a professional marriage counselor. After it was written and arranged so that it might be read in daily sections for a month's period, someone had suggested that it might be of additional value if he would add a Scripture verse and a sentence prayer to each day's selection. Dr. Mace agreed that this might be a good idea. Counselees who used the book might or might not care to use the Scripture verse or the prayer, but the counselor's information and guidance would be there just the same.

When I had made this clear to John and Gloria, to my astonishment John said, "Of course we will be glad to take the books and follow your suggestion." His wife agreed.

One month later the two came back together for their second joint interview. I shall never forget the expression on John's face or his words as he entered the room. He was holding Dr. Mace's little book in his hand and before saying "Good Morning" or any other word of greeting he said, "If this is religion, it is what I have been looking for all my life."

"Why, I didn't give you that as a book of religion, remember, but as a marriage counselor's guidebook."

"Well," John replied, "this did something for me and for my wife, and we are grateful."

This is not the end of this story, but it is enough to show that the Holy Spirit, as I believe, took over in the moment of my frustration and panic. He provided exactly what was necessary for meeting the needs of this couple and breaking through their high walls of defense and resentment toward each other. I do not believe any success would have been possible apart from the Holy Spirit; He provided the inspiration, support, motivation, and direction which this couple needed at that time.

I would not suggest that this kind of experience happens every day, nor do I want to imply that the pastor or counselor may expect such unusual happenings to occur often. But I do suggest that on special occasions, when nothing else will suffice, we are not hopeless or helpless. Relying upon the fulfillment of

Christ's promises through His Holy Spirit, we may be sure that His will will be done through us. We will be given the necessary wisdom to help our counselees. In turn the same Holy Spirit will open their minds and hearts to receive what they need to receive.

From John and Gloria's story we get an illustration of what I have called "inspiration." It has in it both divine and human elements. It comes from above and beyond the knowledge or skill of the counselor, and it gets through to the counselees to bring about constructive results.

7 *PROVIDING*

MOTIVATION

❊❊

Clara had lost her husband in a tragic accident. Left with two small children, she struggled through the years of their childhood and youth to provide a home and an education until both were married and she was left alone. Household duties were uninteresting and at times she was lonely and bored. Life seemed to be behind her with nothing to challenge in the future.

Of course Clara had the usual interest and love for her children and grandchildren, but they lived in other states and she seldom had visits from them. When they did come, they could not remain very long and their visits meant much more work and time spent cooking and cleaning. It was these long days and weeks and months when she was alone that brought her to me for counseling.

Clara needed some interest, some motivation to challenge her and occupy her time usefully. So I listened to her as she recounted phases of her life in the past, seeking always for a clue that might open doors of hope and interest.

Once or twice Clara mentioned how she had always wanted to paint but had never had art lessons. Now she had the time, but that was all. After the second mention, I picked up this hint and asked her if she knew about the local Art Association which was open to any interested person. The membership fee was unbelievably small and the opportunity to share in the interests and activities of neighbors with similar interests might be worth investigating.

There was an art exhibit of the Art Association now on display at the city library, I told Clara, and I happened to know the person in charge who arranged the exhibit. If Clara would like to meet her I would gladly call and arrange a meeting. Clara agreed and I phoned my friend immediately. The result was that Clara became actively interested in learning more about painting through contact with artists who lived in the city, but she also started to paint herself. And since she had exceptional talent, she became a very fine portrait painter.

For a number of years many pastoral counselors felt their task was completed when their counselees gained insight as to their problems. Once a person understood what the problem was, he would then be able to solve it. But unfortunately this had proved to be an error in our thinking. We know that insight is important, but it is not necessarily the cure. Occasionally it is, but often it is not, for there are other important factors which must be considered.

My first thought about this chapter was to omit the idea of motivation altogether. The chapter on inspiration, I felt, would take care of it. But then I realized that there is a difference between the two. Inspiration, on the one hand, lifts a person's sights and holds before him a desire for a solution to his problem. Motivation, on the other hand, provides the necessary fuel to move toward that goal. Inspiration is within the mind and heart, while motivation takes effect in the hands and feet.

Inspiration may be compared to the rejuvenating and reviving effect of a good deep breath of fresh air. Motivation puts this newly inhaled oxygen to work producing action through the muscles.

It is interesting to study the varied instances in which Christ healed persons who sought help from him. There was the man born blind for example. Jesus spat on the ground, made clay, and then put it on the blind man's eyes. This served, no doubt, as a kind of inspiration in that it made the blind man feel that something was definitely being done for him. There was hope that he might yet see. But this was not all. Jesus gave him motivation by telling him to go and wash in the pool of Siloam. Not until he did this were his eyes opened so that he could see (John 9:1–8).

In another instance, people brought to Jesus a man who was paralyzed and confined to his bed, and asked Jesus to heal him. When Jesus saw the faith of the man's friends, He said to the paralytic, "Take heart, my son; your sins are forgiven you." This, of course, created discussion and argument with the scribes who claimed He had no right or power to forgive sins on earth. Therefore He was blaspheming!

But Jesus countered by asking them whether it is easier to say "Your sins are forgiven," or to say "Rise and walk?" Not waiting for their answer He went on, " 'But that you may know that the Son of man has authority on earth to forgive sin,'—he then said to the paralytic—'Rise, take up your bed and go home.' And he rose and went home" (Matt. 9:2–7).

The special feature in this instance is, of course, the relationship between the forgiveness of sins and the healing of physical illness. In modern language we might say that this was a psychosomatic situation. The personality, approach, and confidence of the Master in pronouncing the man's sins to be forgiven reached to the roots of the emotional and spiritual problem and bypassed the physical symptoms. But we also need to see that *after* Jesus gave the man inspiration, He issued a specific command which provided motivation. "Rise, take up your bed, and go home."

In recent pastoral counseling literature I have been made aware of what is called "action therapy," which aims to get the counselee to *do* something rather than merely think through a problem or gain an insight. There are many cases in medical history where motivation resulting in physical effort has been the first step toward healing. Our problem, of course, is to know what motivation to give and how to give it. Each counselee must be dealt with according to his own attitudes and aptitudes. And of course the motivation must be directly related to the desired goal in the counselee's mind and heart.

In each of the illustrations mentioned above it is clear that Jesus understood the desired goals of the counselees. He inspired them to hope that these goals might be achieved, then provided motivation by instructing them to *do* something which required activity or action. But this action was also directly related to the physical symptoms.

For the paralytic who was bedridden and could not walk, the appropriate action was to rise from the bed and to walk, and this was what Jesus instructed him to do. And He added something else. To prove that his arms were strong enough and his limbs had healed sufficiently, he was told to take up his bed and walk—to his own home. What could be a better motivation than this for a paralyzed man. He was to make the effort to get up and walk, and he was to be strong enough to carry his bed. But also he was to go home—the most welcome and desirable place for this man at this time.

In the second incident, I feel there must be some relationship between the question that the disciples asked Jesus regarding the blind man and the belief the man himself had. Perhaps he had learned from his parents and from society that a person is born blind because his parents have sinned and his blindness is a direct punishment. Or else, as the disciples suggested in their question, the man himself had somehow sinned and brought the blindness upon himself.

In the light of Christian theology, neither of these questions need be asked. Through the teaching and example of Christ, we have learned that God does not deal in this manner with His people. To be sure, people may lose their sight through carelessness or even through some actual sin on their part. A child may lose his sight as a result of some physical illness or handicap of his parents, or through something that takes place in the birth process itself. But Christian theology does not think of the blindness as punishment for a sin, nor does it view any handicap as caused directly by some sin. Jesus immediately dispelled this idea from the disciples' minds by saying that the man's blindness was not due to the sin of the man or his parents. No doubt the blind man heard this discussion and thus was made hopeful that something might be accomplished toward regaining his sight. This we would think of as inspiration.

Having provided this inspiration, the Master Counselor proceeded to the next step—the direct physical contact with the blinded eyes. Jesus made a paste with clay and His spittle and put it on the man's eyes, much as a physician today would anoint a person's eyes with some salve which had healing properties. The act also had a psychological value, increasing the man's hope, and preparing him for the next act. Also, if the blindness might have been related to the man's spiritual and emotional conflicts rather than to some organic factor, the anointing with clay would have much the same effect as the doctor's sugar pills have upon a neurotic person who believes that the pills themselves provide the healing or the relief.

The healing did not take place after the blind man had received inspiration. I believe it would not have taken place without the motivation the Master provided which led the man to make some real effort toward healing. So Jesus told him to go and wash in the pool of Siloam. The blind man went and washed, and as a result his sight was restored.

Let us turn to another incident where Jesus counseled the woman whom He met at the well in Samaria (John 4). Her problem was not physical but moral and spiritual. Jesus first intrigued her by asking a favor of her and then talking about water which would keep her from thirsting. When the woman asked for this water so that she would not have to keep returning to the well, Jesus picked up the hint and began gently to probe her problem. The water was a metaphor for spiritual thirst and moral drought, and Jesus sensed the evidences of guilt in her expression. He had inspired her by suggesting that she might have this "living water" which would quench her thirst permanently and be a continual source of satisfaction. Then He motivated her by telling her to go and call her husband and bring him there.

This was indeed a master stroke and an essential step. It threw the focus of attention on the woman, on her own sinfulness which she did not want to admit.

"I have no husband," she said. But Jesus would not accept this. "You are right in saying, 'I have no husband,' for you have had five husbands, and he whom you now have is not your husband; this you said truly."

This was confrontation of the first order, but the woman was still resistant and had up her defenses. She tried her best to turn the counselor's attention away from herself by raising a theological question. She first appealed to His ego by granting Him the status of prophet saying, "Sir, I perceive that you are a prophet." Had He been like some of us counselors today, He would have fallen for this and assumed that now she realized the counselor's worth, and He had a chance to make the most of it. The question she asked of this prophet, as she called Jesus, was regarding the proper place of worship—whether it was to be in Mt. Gerizim nearby in Samaria, or in Jerusalem. This moved the conversation into what appeared to be the spiritual realm, which was the appropriate one for a prophet or pastoral counselor.

Jesus did not reject her question but gave her a specific answer. The place of worship, He said, was not important; she was placing emphasis on that which is unimportant.

"You worship what you do not know." This was a challenge to her theology, but her defenses were gradually falling. He went on to say with confidence, "We worship what we know, for salvation is from the Jews." This turned the attention back to the God of Abraham, Isaac, and Jacob who is the true and only God.

He did not dwell on this point but followed by saying that "the hour is coming, and now is, when the true worshipers will worship the Father in spirit and truth, for such the Father seeks to worship him. God is spirit, and those who worship him must worship in spirit and in truth."

The woman responded by keeping to the theological realm. This is a natural thing for a guilty person to do in the presence of a pastoral counselor—it is intended to give the counselor the impression that the person knows theology and is well informed in its teachings. The woman went on to say, "I know that Messiah is coming; when he comes he will show us all things." Immediately Jesus said, "I who speak to you am he."

This was all the woman could take. She was now so inspired, excited, and hopeful that she was ready to act and act quickly. When the disciples arrived at that moment, they were surprised that Jesus was talking with a woman. But the woman left her water pot, forgetting what she had come to the well for. She went back into the city to tell everyone the good news: "Come, see a man which told me all that I ever did. Can this be the Christ?"

By following along with the woman's trend of thought but lifting it step-by-step to higher and more accurate spiritual levels, Jesus prepared the way for her to take action. Thus when she was convinced emotionally and intellectually that Jesus was the Christ, the Messiah, she was so excited and stimulated that she rushed back to the city, leaving her water pot behind, and spreading the news everywhere.

Many additional illustrations could be found in the New Testament where both Jesus and His disciples made use of the principle of motivation in the process of therapy. There would be value in making a more thorough study of all cases of healing in the New Testament, for each would have in it something to contribute, and to illustrate the importance of providing motivation.

Although this is an important principle in all counseling, it is not always recognized or acted upon. For example, when a person is suffering from grief because of the loss of a loved one, we tend to offer comfort and stop there. Having been with the counselee and family through the initial shock that comes with grief, we may assume that the task is done. Perhaps we make another call or two within the next week or ten days. And then we feel our task is done.

But research in the area of grief counseling shows that there are a number of well-known stages that grief may pass through. And it is possible that a person becomes fixated at one point in the process, and is unable to rise above the grief and adjust to normal living. Comfort and inspiration are valuable and necessary, but they may not be enough. What is lacking for many people in grief is motivation. "What is there now to live for?" a bereaved person sometimes asks. If the pastor or counselor does not recognize this fact or fails to follow through, the emotional state of the counselee may go from bad to worse.

It is at this point that the pastoral counselor must do his best to discover an appropriate, available, and useful task or course of action to prescribe. It is his responsibility to suggest some definite activity which will bring the person out of the loneliness and solitude of grief and withdrawal back into relationships with other people.

To illustrate, let me take a case out of the files and see how this principle operates. Mrs. Andrews was referred to me by a pastor who said that she had not been able to adjust following the drowning death of her husband, which had occurred some months before. The pastor was at his wit's end, he said, and she needed help. What could be done?

Of course I could not give him a ready-made answer, but after several interviews which were used to provide empathy and catharsis, I saw clearly that along with the grief was unresolved guilt. She had been warned some years before by her husband, who had had a heart attack while in swimming, that he should not take this risk.

On the occasion of his death, however, the two of them were in a boat. It was such a beautiful day and so comfortably warm, that she encouraged and really dared him to dive in with her and swim. After some hesitation he did so, but quickly he went under the water and did not come up. Mrs. Andrews was convinced that she had killed her husband. In addition, however, she also had guilt feelings leading back further into the marriage. She felt that she had failed her husband in many ways, having rejected him time after time sexually.

I listened patiently and actively to all the details of her husband's death and of their unhappy moments in marriage. She now felt the unhappiness had been due largely to her own wrong attitude. I began by providing such encouragement and inspiration as I could. I tried to show her that, regardless of her failures and sinfulness, we have a God who has promised that if we confess our sins, He is faithful and just to forgive them and to cleanse us from all unrighteousness.

Furthermore, I reminded her that God has promised to remove our transgressions from us as far as the east is from the west and to remember them against us no more forever. And Jesus Christ forgave the sins of the people who came to Him and taught the availability of full pardon to the repentant sinner. The Apostle Peter denied his Lord after swearing that he would die with Him rather than deny Him, but Jesus forgave him. This last illustration gave me the cue for the next step in her recovery. Motivation was needed. She must *do* something now; not just think, feel, and confess—but act.

Was not this what Jesus did with Peter when He asked him three times if he loved Him? Each time Peter insisted that his Master was dear to him, thought he could not claim to have the depth and quality of love that he should have for Him. Each time Jesus prescribed *action:* "Feed my lambs," "Feed my sheep," and again "Feed (shepherd) my sheep." Here was a definite task which required action on Peter's part and was essential to his full recovery from guilt.

So with Mrs. Andrews, I led her to see the necessity of going further than she had gone and taking some definite, positive, and constructive action. The type of action which would be best, I suggested, would be volunteering some service that was needed in the church or in the community. Even the story of her life, her failures, and her grief could be put to use on occasion. She could furnish guidelines to others lost in the same fog and darkness of despair. Surely there were those around whom she knew were suffering to some degree as she was. Had she thought of cultivating a relationship with them for the purpose of providing guidance such as she had received and which could lead them out of their unhappy condition?

Her response was, "Yes, I do know someone who has had a similar experience, and you think that perhaps I could help her?"

"Yes, indeed," I replied, "and why not?"

And so it was that Mrs. Andrews received her motivation to take action. Eventually she was led back into a normal relationship with her friends and neighbors in the community as well as in the church.

In summary, let us remember that although helping a person gain insight and inspiration is important, we must not stop there. To be genuinely effective, counseling must motivate the counselee to action. This is another way of saying that counselees need a purpose for living. They must see that life has a meaning which is worthwhile and hence worth effort.

The wise counselor will attempt to provide some specific guidance and suggestions as to the type of action which the counselee must undertake. The act must be something that is appropriate to the counselee's need, something within the realm of possible achievement, and specific enough for the counselee to understand and begin to do. The counselor needs creative imagination here, combined with his understanding of the counselee, who needs to agree with the counselor on a definite plan of action to begin promptly.

The psychological principle that operates here was stated by William James in speaking of habit formation. If a person wants to form a new habit, he needs to do three things: (1) begin as promptly as possible; (2) repeat as often as possible; and (3) allow as few exceptions to occur as possible. Thus the counselor will need to follow through with the counselee until the proposed action becomes well established or habitual.

8. SOME WHO FOUND
PURPOSE

〰〰〰〰〰〰〰〰〰〰〰〰〰〰〰〰〰〰〰〰〰〰〰〰〰〰〰〰

Peter was 25 and slightly overweight when he came in for counseling. He belonged to a very prominent family, and he had failed prep school. This was so out of character compared to the other members of the family that he was sure they were ashamed of him. Actually, his father, who had a well-known and successful business, had made it quite clear that he never expected Peter to be able to follow him in the business; Peter lacked both the education and the intelligence required for success.

Peter had been married and divorced—a very unhappy situation. His parents before him were divorced, and his father had married for the second time. Peter's sister was very brilliant— she had her problems but never in the intellectual realm. However, she too seemed to have more pity than appreciation for him, for he was not prepared to make a living and did not seem to have the slightest idea what he could do.

After I had established good rapport with Peter, and given him acceptance and understanding and a degree of appreciation of his sincerity and potential, he seemed quite willing to pursue my suggestion. Aptitude tests showed that he might succeed in a specialized field which did not require a college education. This work could be quite remunerative depending upon the amount of skill he would develop.

I learned that a two-year course was being offered in the city, and since Peter had some G. I. funds as yet unused, he enrolled.

Although there were times when I wondered if he would continue, Peter finished the course and set up his own business to the joy, delight, and surprise of his entire family.

During my years in pastoral counseling, I have dealt with many types of counselees and a wide variety of problems. Some basic principles and procedures, such as outlined in earlier chapters in this book, are to some degree repeated in almost every instance. But each case is also unique. In this chapter I would like to present a number of counseling situations and illustrations. I hope these will provide some practical suggestions and help counselors discover ways and means of motivating the people who come to them for help.

A CASE OF PARALYSIS

Mrs. Henry had had two strokes of paralysis which had left her with no control of her right arm and only slight control of her left leg. By leaning heavily on a cane, she managed to get around her home and do what was necessary to maintain her existence. She lived alone—her son at this time was in service during the Korean conflict.

She was a member of my congregation, and I discovered when I called on her that not only was she terribly lonely but she also felt that she was useless and that life was meaningless. She had not been doing any reading and could not write, and therefore spent most of her time simply watching television.

After a series of interviews, during which I followed the usual steps in counseling, including such inspiration as I was able to offer, I was face-to-face with the problem of motivation. How could a person so handicapped be motivated to *do* anything that would be very useful or challenging?

Much thought and prayer led me finally to ask if Mrs. Henry would be interested in helping me with my counseling ministry? Would she like to make a scrapbook of appropriate clippings from magazines which would be useful in the variety of problems which various counselees have and with which I must deal? Mrs. Henry expressed amazement that I thought she could do anything worthwhile, but if there was anything she could do, she said, she would be most happy to do it. The result was that she was motivated to read as she had not done for years. Later she told me that I had saved her mind by giving her some way to keep it occupied and alive.

Even after I left this pastorate, Mrs. Henry continued to send me loose-leaf notebooks filled with clippings and indexed. The clippings were crudely cut out because she was right handed, and her right arm was useless. The index was typed with one finger. I have fourteen such volumes; they kept her busy over a number of years and have added a great deal of useful material to my counseling library.

AN ULCER CASE

When Mr. Williams came for counseling, he did so upon the insistence of both his employer and his doctor. His doctor was convinced that Mr. Williams' ulcer was caused by his emotional condition. He was an engineer of the first order, designing new instruments for the large manufacturing concern by whom he was employed, and had a number of draftsmen and designers working under him. I learned later that he had made the highest academic average that had ever been made at the prominent school of technology from which he had graduated. There was no question as to his competency or his efficiency. But he had a mortal fear of losing his job and was unable even to go to lunch with men in his department because he was so nauseated when lunch time came that he ate his sandwiches alone.

It became very evident to me that Mr. Williams' anxiety and the threat to his security had generated in him a deeply hostile attitude toward both his employer and his immediate superior in the company. This superior, he said, was "breathing down his neck"—he came in every morning and looked over his shoulder at his work. Mr. Williams' hostility did not show up in the office. He did not lose his temper there, though he did become very demanding of those who worked under him.

His real hostility showed up when he went home. He yelled at his wife and children if a closet door was left ajar or if anything was out of order. His son could never please him with his school grades, and on one occasion ran away from home. His wife was ready to seek a divorce, saying that she could not live with him because he was so demanding and irritable.

Part of Mr. Williams' hostility was also caused by his assuming a greater financial responsibility than his income readily allowed. He felt he must have a new house next door to his superior's which would be equally as fine a home. He had to be at work, he thought, thirty minutes before anyone else in the office and would remain thirty minutes after all had left, to prove that he was doing his job well. He was compulsive to the extreme—and under it all was the hostility.

When we reached the point where motivation was indicated I made what may seem to be a very trite suggestion.

"You must find some way to work off that hostility," I told him—"a way that is harmless to yourself, your family, and your job. Since you are fighting mad, I wonder if you couldn't make good use of a punching bag located somewhere out of hearing distance from your family, perhaps in the garage or down in the basement? When you come home each day, imagine that the punching bag is the one against whom you are most angry and give it some severe blows as long as you feel like doing so."

Mr. Williams took the suggestion. His daily punching sessions had a miraculous effect upon his condition. His ulcer, under the medical care it was having, healed, and his efficiency at the office was improved. He was now able to be more relaxed and less compulsive and demanding. His superior also, after a conversation with me, became aware of the threat he had been. Instead of "breathing down his neck" every day, he found ways to commend Mr. Williams for his good work.

WIFE OF AN ALCOHOLIC

Mrs. Stephens had had several interviews regarding her marriage which she said was falling apart because her husband had recently begun drinking, and she could not tolerate drinking. Mr. Stephens would not come with her to see me, and did not know that she had come—he would be very angry if he knew.

In one of the interviews Mrs. Stephens said that when she came home from work one afternoon she found her husband sitting in the corner of a room with an empty whiskey bottle beside him on the floor and giving orders to two Negro women who were on their hands and knees waxing and polishing the floor. She became very angry and let him know it. Whenever he got drunk, she told me she felt like going out of the house and never seeing him again. Usually she did leave the room and stayed away from him as long as possible until he sobered up.

I asked her if she felt that alcoholism was a sickness. Yes, she did. What would she do about her husband, I asked, if he came home with a heart attack or a bad case of the flu.

"Oh," she said, "I would do everything I could to get him to bed as quickly as possible."

"I wonder what would happen if you treated your husband as a sick person the next time he comes home drunk and did all you could do to help him get to bed?"

Well, she didn't know and wasn't sure that she could do it, but maybe she could try.

An interview or two later she told me what had happened the next time he came in drunk.

"I felt like going out of the house as usual, but then I remembered your suggestion. I decided I would try it." Mr.

Stephens had flopped down in a chair in the living room. She went over to him, showing as much concern as she could, and began taking off his shoes and helping him to get to bed. This was something entirely new for him.

"Who have you been talking to?" he asked, looking up in his drunken state.

Fearing to tell him that she had been seeking counseling, she replied, "Nobody!"

"Oh, yes you have," he countered.

"What makes you think so?"

"Because now you are back on my side."

Mr. Stephens voluntarily came with his wife to the next interview and began seeking counseling for himself. I gave both of them a series of inventory tests. When they discovered how similar their needs were, they were greatly surprised. Neither had much self-confidence. Both felt extremely inadequate. As they began working toward more understanding of themselves and of each other, they were led to a closer relationship and mutual acceptance and love.

In this case two suggestions were made which provided motivation: (1) that the wife begin treating her drunken husband as a sick person; and (2) that both of them take a battery of inventories to gain a better understanding of themselves. Both actions were essential to a successful outcome in this case.

AN ESTRANGED COUPLE

Mr. and Mrs. Bruce came in for a joint interview. Mr. Bruce was madly chewing on an unlighted cigar and in every way indicated that he was very angry and greatly disturbed. Mrs. Bruce was a very attractive person. Both were in their middle forties.

As their story unfolded it became evident that Mr. Bruce's outstanding business success, which had provided every conceivable material comfort for his family, had brought no happiness.

Mrs. Bruce indicated very forcibly that it was not his money she wanted. She wanted "him!" He had been too busy and often too tired to give her the time and attention she so much needed. Now, Mrs. Bruce had found a man who was very, very thoughtful and who made her feel like the woman she wanted to be. She and this man were corresponding. Her husband had discovered one of these "love letters" and was both hurt and hostile.

The hostility was so great that I was forced to arrange for separate interviews. They could not discuss their problems in the presence of each other. I scheduled the next interview with Mrs. Bruce.

She began by telling me how thoughtful her husband had been when he was courting her. Among other thoughtful things he did, she said, he always brought one or more roses to her whenever he came for a date. He had not done such a "sweet thing" since they were married. Then she mentioned a number of other illustrations of his consideration and thoughtfulness which he had not repeated since marriage.

During this interview Mrs. Bruce indicated that she hesitated to mention such "trivial" things, but that they did mean much to her. They had become symbols of her husband's love. And it certainly would do no good to their relationship at this point if I told him what she had said. He would only go through the "act" without the thoughtful initiative which he formerly took and which convinced her of his love. So I had to promise her that I would not mention a single one of the things she mentioned to him. I promised that I would only remind him that he once found ways to show his love for her, that these had become the language of love to her, and that they would always hold such a place in her mind and heart.

When Mr. Bruce arrived for the next interview, he immediately asked me what his wife had told me. I replied that I had promised her that I would not repeat anything she had said. This enraged him, and he almost left the counseling room.

"What good did it do to talk with her if you can't tell me anything she said that would help our marriage?"

My reply was a simple one, but it proved to be sufficient to motivate Mr. Bruce in the right direction and to lead him to effective action.

"Mr. Bruce, before you were married you managed to find ways to convince Mrs. Bruce that you loved her and that she could trust you to understand her needs and desires and meet them. Think back, now, and try to recall just what you did to win your wife."

That was all I said. He agreed to try this assignment and said he would return for the interview which we set up following another one with his wife.

Something happened that made it necessary for Mrs. Bruce to postpone her scheduled interview. I suggested that she arrange with Mr. Bruce to come when he was supposed to come and for him to postpone his interview until afterwards. But on the day scheduled, to my surprise, they arrived together. On their faces was a new expression. It was of relief and love rather than of hostility and resentment.

"What has happened to you two?" I asked.

The question triggered a series of efforts on the part of each to get the other to answer. Finally, with a bit of embarrassment and some hesitation Mrs. Bruce spoke.

"Well," she began, "John has been the sweetest thing lately! He's been like the John I married!" After a pause she continued: "Since we were here last he has done so many thoughtful little things. He seemed never to come home at night that he hadn't brought some little thoughtful token of his love or called during the day to see how I was and what I was doing. It has been like the way he did when we were going together before we married. I'm sure there never was a husband who can think of so many nice ways to show his wife that he thinks about her no matter how busy he is at the office!

"For instance, some nights he would bring home a rosebud

he picked up from the florist on the corner near his office. Then, the other night—Saturday night—he brought me a dozen beautiful yellow rosebuds! It seemed like we were back in those wonderful days of courtship when life seemed so happy and bright!"

Thus, a bit of appropriate motivation led this couple to take specific steps toward working through their difficulties. Throughout my relationship with the Bruces, I was aware of the guiding and directing hand of One who understood this couple far better than I did.

A "SMOTHERED" SON

Joel Daniels, the twenty-one year old son of a university professor, had failed in his effort to go through college. His parents were embarrassed and ashamed of his failure and had concluded that he wasn't very bright. The young man was equally uncertain about his mental capacity and had decided that he was doomed to failure in life. Even his efforts in dating the girls had failed to work out to any degree of satisfaction.

The Daniels had two sons, and Joel was the younger of the two, but both seemed to lack either ambition or ability academically. However, Mrs. Daniels "loved" them very much and every night she literally tucked them in bed as she had done since they were small children. The older son was able to fool his mother. She was constantly giving him money for his varied "adventures," none of which proved financially successful.

Joel, however, could not "manufacture" adequate excuses to secure funds from his mother, nor was he ever convinced that she cared as much for him as she did for his brother who bore his mother's proud family name. So he came to me for counseling.

When good empathy was established and I had listened for hours to his many attempts which had all resulted in failure, I suggested that we give him some aptitude tests. The result of these led me to conclude that his potential lay in the direction of restaurant work, so I suggested that he inquire about training in this type of business.

By reason of the confidence I had built in our relationship, Joel took my suggestion and soon reported that a restaurant chain manager in the city had encouraged him to come in for training.

As the weeks merged into months, Joel became interested in a fine young woman who seemed to appreciate him and encourage him in his undertaking. Soon they were married, and he was made assistant manager of one of the restaurants. This gave him a new image of himself, and his family a new attitude toward him. Since then the years have brought to him several promotions and a degree of usefulness and success.

Perhaps you will have noticed that I made no direct reference to the Holy Spirit in the last two cases. The apparent omission was deliberate. By this I intended to point out an underlying fact which I believe is important. I do not feel it is always necessary to say that I am always aware of my own limitations. On the other hand, I work on the belief that God is constantly operating in my work and through my thoughts, leading me to discover ways and means of motivating counselees to put their new insights and knowledge into action.

I sincerely believe that it is possible to be guided by the ever-present Counselor without always directly addressing Him for such aid. This is as real and practical as it is to "pray without ceasing," which we are told to do in the Scriptures. Such a command does not mean that prayer is to occupy our consciousness every minute of the day, but I am confident that one may live in the spirit of prayer at all times. This means that one has the continual conviction that his personal needs and limitations cannot be overcome apart from direct relationship with God through the work of His Holy Spirit.

I believe that the Christian counselor who humbly and sincerely acknowledges his needs and limitations in this all-important task may rely continually on the guidance of the Wonderful Counselor by the very acknowledgment of this need. To be in "partnership" with Him as the "Senior Counselor" makes the relationship constant and permanent.

9. THE NEED FOR
SPIRITUAL CHANGE

><><><><><><><><><><><><><><><><><><><><><><><><><><><><><><

If the pastoral counselor is genuinely concerned about seeing a permanent change take place in his counselee, then that change must take place within the counselee's area of basic viewpoints and attitudes. By this I mean that something must happen to him at a "depth" level which I call the "spiritual" level. The theological term for this change would be conversion or new birth. I feel that often the temptation of the pastoral counselor has been to stay clear of this area, in order to maintain the more "scientific" or "objective" relationship to the counselee which the psychologically or sociologically oriented counselor rightfully and necessarily seeks.

I find no fault with psychologically or sociologically oriented counselors. Rather I admire and respect them for drawing a clear-cut line where their training ends and the training of the theologically oriented counselor begins. Actually they do the ethically correct thing for them, just as the minister counselor or pastoral counselor does the correct thing in drawing a clear-cut line between his counseling limitations and those that would require the specialized training of the physician, clinical psychologist, psychiatrist, or sociologist.

I realize, of course, that it is difficult to draw such clear-cut lines of differentiation. But if we allow these limits to be obscured or to become fuzzy, we may do our counselees a disservice and also subject ourselves and the pastoral profession to justifiable criticism. Actually this would become malpractice in the case of the pastoral counselor, just as I feel it is malpractice for the psychiatrist, clinical psychologist, or sociologist to enter deeply into the theological field in counseling when he is poorly prepared to do so. I am fully aware of the overlapping of these fields to a degree, but still there must be limits somewhere, and each person must determine these limits for himself, based upon his own background of experience and training.

Ideally it would be well if every pastor could have adequate psychological, psychiatric, and sociological training so that all such limits would be removed. But practically this seems in most cases to be impossible. Each of these fields is so extensive and demands such thorough and intensive training that the ordinary period allowed for one's formal education is far too short for a pastor to obtain all of these qualifications. Much of his life's span would be used up before he reached the point where he was ready to do actual counseling in the workaday world.

Assuming that some counselees do need a basic change in depth in their entire viewpoint and direction of life (best described as a "new birth" or "regeneration"), who is to perform the counseling in this area if the pastoral counselor neglects to? Who else has had the privilege and opportunity of depth training in the spiritual realm in which regeneration must necessarily take place? Who else has the opportunity to deal with this area to the degree the pastor has? In many cases he has been chosen by the very people whom he serves to be their pastor because they admire, respect, and trust him; they feel that his training and life equip him for doing this particular task.

Admittedly, few men feel they can measure up to the high and often impossible standards set by parishioners for their pastor. Hence out of justifiable humility pastors become rather hesitant in assuming such a high function. But right here lies a great danger for both the pastor and those whom he serves. In order to avoid becoming a hypocrite or compromising with his own personal integrity he may become too hesitant and over-cautious about undertaking these deeper and more spiritual relationships with counselees.

The opposite danger, however, is that a pastor may outwardly accept the image that his people create for him, and may attempt to perform on that level. The result is often tragic. Eventually he will be discovered to be human rather than the perfect or completely mature person that some of his people want him to be. Having posed as the ideal person in the presence of his people he must continually wear a mask or put up an artificial front.

The psychological effect on the pastor is to make him suppress or repress his real self in public and then release his hostility in the safer environment of his home and in the presence of his family. The natural result is a feeling of guilt which makes him more and more reluctant to become emotionally involved on a spiritual level with his counselee, lest his Achilles' heel be discovered and his image and usefulness be destroyed.

What I am saying here is simply this. The pastor must first of all be a real person so that he does not need to wear a mask. He will run the risk of being misunderstood, criticized, or sometimes even rejected by certain insecure persons who have a neurotic need to imagine him as perfect and to lean upon him. To discover that he, too, has limitations and weaknesses can be so threatening and disillusioning to these persons that he can no longer be the leader and helper that they want him to be. This may seem an unfortunate result. But there is another angle we need to examine. Allowing a person to become more and more dependent weakens rather than strengthens him. It only makes the neurotic person more neurotic.

Here we are confronted, I suppose, with one of the most difficult aspects of the pastor's life and ministry—knowing and being himself in the presence of his parishioners. How can he take this risk? What will be the results if he dares to do so? Can the blind lead the blind, or the lame help the lame to walk? The answer would naturally be "of course not." On the other hand, what we need to recognize and accept is that there are degrees of blindness and lameness to which all of us are subject due to our basic humanity with its inbred flaws and limitations. Try as we may, we find ourselves restricted on every hand by inheritance and environment, and these are powerful influences upon us. On the surface it would seem that we are helpless victims in the hands of such powerful forces. And we are, from the human standpoint. But it is at this point that our Christian faith makes the difference.

The Christian is taught that he "cannot save himself," he cannot "lift himself by his own boot straps." Millions of people have attempted this through countless centuries, but to no avail. Only Jesus Christ, the Man of Galilee, according to Christian teaching, did not need to lift himself by His own boot straps. He is the only person in history who was "tempted in all points as we are yet without sin." Hence He becomes our Ideal and Model as well as our Hope.

Having used the words ideal and model, I hasten to add another point which I sincerely believe. We all need an ideal and model around which to formulate our aims and goals in life. But having an ideal is a far cry from being able to achieve its standards. Of course, many would argue that just trying to achieve the ideal is worth it. I would agree that this is true. But if this is the totality of our hope, then we are doomed to frustration, disappointment, and to a degree, failure. I say this from my own personal experience. But I also can readily refer to the pages of history and biography to provide an abundance of evidence that even the strongest men and women, apart from this Man of Galilee, have failed to achieve their ideal. That is, I can find no other person on the pages of history or in the volumes of biography who has attained perfection in his daily life. Especially is this true when we look below the surface to motives, thoughts, and attitudes.

If perfection of ideal and image demands that the apple be sound from surface to core, or rather from action to motive and thought beneath the surface, our problem becomes even more real and difficult. If what Jesus of Nazareth said is true, that "everyone who looks at a woman lustfully has already committed adultery with her in his heart," or if "anyone who hates his brother is a murderer," who, I ask, can honestly claim to be perfect, free from all such thoughts? If it is true that "as a man thinks in his heart so is he," then we must find a man whose thoughts are above reproach at all times, in order to find a man who is faultless at all times. What pastor can justifiably make such a claim and sustain it in the light of the penetrating rays of justice, mercy, and truth?

If none but the perfectly mature and adequate person is to counsel in this deeper level of the spiritual, counseling would be impossible. We would be completely frustrated in a search for such a person, because there is no one who has reached this level of performance. Hence the spiritual would never be dealt with in the counseling relationship.

Although a pastor is limited by his performance and behavior, we can find no person and no profession as well qualified to enter into this spiritual relationship. But the pastor as a person must first be honest with himself and with his God before he can be honest with his people. This kind of honesty can only occur when he himself has experienced a genuine "conversion" or "new birth"—when he has experienced "regeneration."

We could get into an endless and hopeless discussion if we tried to determine to what degree this regeneration is a result of man's effort on the one hand and of God's intervention on the other. I hope that we shall be delivered from this controversy. It seems to me that both are involved. We need to recognize that man has a degree of responsibility. But regardless of his willingness or ability to assume this responsibility, I am convinced that apart from the spiritual intervention of the Holy Spirit the end results will be frustrating.

I believe that the regeneration—the new birth or conversion —of the pastoral counselor, like that of his counselees, must result from the dual encounter with self and with the Holy Spirit. Any transformation of the spiritual aspect of man must be related directly and intimately to the source of spiritual power. This power I believe is found only in a God who Himself is Spirit and who, through the statements of the Holy Scriptures, encounters men in the spiritual realm through the work of the Holy Spirit.

In other words, the pastoral counselor himself must experience regeneration. Only when this encounter has taken place, and the pastor as a person has responded fully to it and to the Holy Spirit, can he be set free from the fears which would cause him to wear a mask or put up a false front.

The pastor's reliance must be upon God rather than upon himself. A genuine reliance will become increasingly evident to to those whom he touches in the counseling relationship, because of his genuine humility, courage, hope, and faith, as well as the quality and depth of his love. These qualities are "fruits of the Spirit." Only to the degree that they become genuine in our daily lives are we pastors able to be effective on the spiritual level in our counseling relationships. If we are not guided and controlled by this Spirit from God, we are to a large degree incapacitated, limited to dealing with our counselees on the superficial level and avoiding their spiritual needs.

If my words have been interpreted as demanding perfection, then I have been misunderstood. What I am appealing for is spiritual genuineness rather than behavioral perfection. The truly regenerated pastor need make no claim to perfection.

Rather because of the inner security he now has, he of all men is most able to admit his limitations and weaknesses, and thus lay proper claim to kinship with his counselees.

Measured by the highest standards of perfection, most of us could truly say with the Apostle Paul that we are "chief of sinners." Having had perhaps the greatest privilege and opportunity of becoming aware of the length, breadth, depth, and height of the perfection and love of God in Christ, we are best able to recognize the many degrees by which we fall short of His standards. Much privilege brings much responsibility.

The truly regenerated person makes no claim to be sinless. His one and only claim is that he does not "want" or "desire" to sin. No one is eager to admit his weaknesses, limitations and the fact of his sinfulness. But the regenerated person is most eager to be forgiven and to receive strength to resist the temptations which lead him to sin. No Christian can honestly say that he has already attained to the high standard set for him by God when we are told to be perfect even as He also is perfect. If he is honest, he can only say, as the Apostle said:

> I do not claim that I have already succeeded in this, or have already become perfect. I keep going on to try to possess it, for Christ Jesus has already possessed me. Of course, brothers, I really do not think that I have already reached it; my single purpose in life, however, is to forget what is behind me and do my best to reach what is ahead. So I run straight toward the goal in order to win the prize, which is God's call through Christ Jesus to the life above.[1]

Undergirded by this faith, one need not pose as something he is not. The direction which his regeneration has laid out for him is *"toward* perfection"—a direction which will not permit him either to stand still or go backward very long. His conscience now has been awakened and his faith strengthened, so that he

---

[1] Phil. 3:12–14, *Good News for Modern Man. The New Testament in Today's English Version.*

knows that when he does sin, genuine and complete forgiveness is available from God by reason of the cross of Christ. Thus, in humble reliance upon the validity and promise of his Heavenly Father, in Christ the Christian may lift up his downcast eyes and again look his fellow men in the face. He is forgiven though not yet perfect; he is facing in the direction of perfection without making the slightest claim that he has already achieved this perfection.

The "regenerated" pastoral counselor, while not claiming to be the only person so qualified, is now in a position to minister to his counselees on the deeper levels of the spiritual. He presents to them through his very life and character a living illustration of the possibility of the counselee's experiencing such regeneration. Not until the pastoral counselor has experienced this release and achieved this sense of security is he ready to provide real regenerative help to others. Now he is in a position to "witness" to that which he himself knows from experience.

Again let me repeat: We must not confuse the experience of regeneration with the claim to perfection. We may still be "babes in Christ" as compared with the ultimate maturity in the spiritual life we may achieve only after years of experience and growth. But even a young child soon becomes aware of his personal relationship to his father and mother and knows to whom he belongs, what his family is, and what name he bears. He knows what rights he has as a child of the family. Depending on the quality of the family, he has no need to be apologetic or feel insecure as to who he is, nor to be afraid or ashamed of other people's knowing these facts about him.

So the pastor who has experienced this new birth, knows who he is and whose name he has the right to bear (not because he earned that right but because he was born into it). Thus he may justly function upon the basis of his relationship to his Father through Christ. He may freely and gladly bear witness to these facts and introduce his counselees to Him who is ready to adopt them also as His children.

The privileges and benefits as well as the honors that accompany this royal relationship are available to everyone. But many people suffer and struggle through life as paupers and worse than paupers because they do not know. They have never experienced a personal confrontation with God who is indeed King of kings and Lord of lords, or come to know Him as their Father.

I feel that the pastoral counselor has the advantage over his fellow counselor who may not have had the privilege of experiencing and forming this relationship with God. The pastor stands at the entrance of the vast world of the spiritual which, I believe, underlies, undergirds, and lifts one above the fatal frustrations and hopeless limitations that inevitably exist in the merely human or material world. If the pastor really believes this, is he not derelict in his duty to his counselee if he either ignores or rejects his responsibility in the spiritual realm? Who else, by virtue of his professional training, will enter into this facet of human life and experience?

Of course such an undertaking is frightening and even threatening if a person should try to go it alone. But if we actually believe that there is present and available the wisdom, guidance, and power of God in His Holy Spirit and that we are not expected to go it alone, then must we not recognize and accept this as a part of our counseling responsibility?

10. PROVIDING OPPORTUNITY
FOR SPIRITUAL CHANGE

XXXXXXXXXXXXXXXXXXXXXXXXXXXXXXXXXXXXXXXXXXXXXXXXXX

The story Harriet told me that day was filled with guilt and shame. She had been sexually promiscuous for years. She had a son, now grown and married, and had never really had a home for the daughter she loved. Vulgarity, profanity and dishonesty had been her way of life through the years. Never before had she had the courage or desire to seek counseling help.

Just the other day, however, a government auditor had discovered rather large discrepancies in her books which she kept for a person of highly questionable character. She was guilty of cooperating with his shrewd and dishonest practices and now was terribly afraid of discovery and imprisonment. What could she do?

Through the process of catharsis, to which I responded with genuine concern and acceptance, Harriet reached the point where she suggested her making a clean breast of it all—she was willing to take the consequences. Since she had found acceptance by me, she said, and through me by God, she was no longer afraid. Now she really *wanted* to make restitution, and set about doing all she could to this end. Never before had she felt like a person who might become "somebody"—useful to society.

The years that have followed have provided amazing evidence of the complete change of her whole attitude toward God and man. Her simple faith has brought about a chain of circumstances almost beyond belief. So much has happened in such a short time to make a real person out of one who was in the depths of sin and despair. For ten years she has remained stable and true.

It is often difficult to be certain that regeneration has actually taken place in a person. But in order to illustrate the principles set forth in the last chapter, I have chosen a few counseling experiences which appear to show such a depth change, with the hope that my judgment is correct. Because deep spiritual changes take place in the secret places of the mind and heart, they are often difficult to detect from outside. And external appearances are not necessarily positive proof that permanent changes have taken place. Therefore, I present the following with this realization and the hope that my readers may understand and profit from these cases.

One of the first principles I follow is the principle of psychological readiness. By this I mean that the counselee must indicate some interest in entering into the spiritual level before I can hope to accomplish any constructive ends. Otherwise I may alienate him. If I feel compelled in every instance to press the spiritual factor in counseling, regardless of the person's psychological readiness, I may find that the first interview may be the last opportunity for counseling the individual.

On the other hand when a counselee indicates in some way that he is seeking something more than scientific or psychological aid, I need to recognize this readiness and respond appropriately. The indication of such readiness may come in many forms. Sometimes it will be an expression of desperation or despair. Sometimes it takes the form of a question such as, "Do you think God would disapprove of what I have done?" Sometimes it may be a mere expression of interest or curiosity— "What do you believe about God and how He looks on this kind of conduct of mine?"

There are many ways in which counselees give a signal, even though often a very weak one, which means, "I came to you because you are a man of God; I feel the need of some guidance, forgiveness, or help from a higher Source than man." Any indication must be recognized as such by the counselor who is then justified in assuming that the troubled person has some awareness of the spiritual aspect of his problem.

There are times when no such signal seems to be forthcoming, but even then the counselor may feel convinced that the counselee will never really be set free or released until he has a personal confrontation with God. In such cases it is often possible for the counselor tactfully but sincerely to open the door which may lead into the deeper level of the spiritual in counseling. He may do this by saying something like the following: "Of course you know I am a minister, and you would expect me to have some kind of faith which you may think of as religious or spiritual. Actually I do have this kind of faith, and in my own experience am convinced that it is valid for me. I also believe that I have seen its validity in relation to helping others face their situations and solve their problems."

At times I have felt that the door was ajar by information secured in the initial interview which informs me that the counselee is a member of certain denomination or is affiliated with a certain church or synagogue. I have found even this slight indication of spiritual readiness to be sufficient indication to allow me to proceed gradually into the spiritual aspects of the counseling relation. Let me pause here to give an example.

On one occasion a series of rather intensive interviews appeared to have come to a dead end. The couple were of a very different faith from mine—they were members of the Conservative Jewish Synagogue of our community. Recognizing this fact and respecting their right to their own faith I had not imposed upon them my Christian views. However, we had come to an impasse. Sarah had not spoken to her mother-in-law in over a year, and the mother-in-law would not speak to her. Sarah insisted that until her mother-in-law apologized to her she would not apologize to her mother-in-law. In the meantime she had forbidden the children to see their grandmother. All this, naturally, produced tremendous tension in Bernie as well as resentment toward both women for placing him in the middle.

"It seems then that your situation has reached a dead end," I said finally to Sarah. "However, I can think of one possible alternative which is suggested to me by one of the teachings of our Christian faith which I fear we do not practice often enough but which I have seen work in one or two cases previously.

"The teaching is that if one's enemy hungers he is to feed him; if he is thirsty he is to give him something to drink. In this way he heaps coals of fire on his head. That means that he melts him down into a friend."

There was a slight smile and then she said, "Would you mind telling me more?"

So I told her about one person I had known who was hostile toward a former friend to the point that neither of them had spoken to each other for thirteen years. I had suggested that she try this melting process and had given her some specific suggestions. She found that it worked. By finding a way to help her "enemy," she broke down all barriers; the two were brought together as the most intimate of friends.

"This is interesting," was Sarah's response, "but I don't know if I could do it with my mother-in-law."

"Well of course, that's up to you," I replied. "I merely mentioned it as a possibility."

In our next interview Sarah told me of a new development.

"I'm disturbed because my mother-in-law goes to the hospital tomorrow for an exploratory operation," she said, "and the doctors seem to think it is possible that she may not live through it. I know it would please my husband if I could go to the hospital and wish her well, but I am sure she would insult me."

We discussed her suggestion from the standpoint of what it could do for their relationship along the lines of the Christian principles I had pointed out and illustrated previously. Finally, with a little support, she said, "I think I'll try it."

A day or two later, after the operation was over, and her mother-in-law had lived through it, husband and wife came to see me hand in hand with smiles on their faces and gratitude in their hearts. Sarah had gone to the hospital to wish her mother-in-law well, and her mother-in-law had broken down and asked forgiveness for the way she had treated Sarah during the past months. This in turn brought forth an apology from Sarah. Their relationship was sealed and has become stronger since then. The reconciliation of the two women also healed the marriage rift, and the gratitude which this couple showed in many ways during the following months and years seemed out of all proportion to the little I as a counselor had been able to do.

What happened was not my work. I was merely using the effective approach that Christ had set forth. The Holy Spirit had taken this and worked with it in the hearts of this couple, and in their relationship to the mother-in-law. In other words the Holy Spirit was working in the home and family of people who had made no profession of faith in Christ; nevertheless they found that this simple Christian principle worked.

Months later I was standing in line to buy tickets for the movie *Ben Hur,* when suddenly someone grasped my arm. It was Bernie, and again he said that he was so glad to see me. "We too are going to see *Ben Hur,* the story of the Christ," he told me. Somehow I feel that God's Spirit worked in a redemptive way with them.

I have used another approach in some situations to turn the interview toward the spiritual. When I have known that a counselee had some active interest in or connection with a Christian church, I would open the interview as usual. After listening to the statement of their problem in some detail, I would comment that this seemed to be a very complex or difficult problem. I laid no claim to superior wisdom or ability to lead them to discover a solution, I would tell them, but I had confidence in "the Senior partner" in my counseling service, namely the Holy Spirit. I believed He could enable us to find the best possible solution. I have tried not to speak in an overly pious tone or in a "preaching" manner, but have made such a statement very naturally and simply because of my sincere belief in its truth.

It has been amazing at times to see what effect this has had. It has prepared the way for future references of a spiritual nature which seemed appropriate at the moment. It has also provided a basis for encouragement and support when the counseling relationship seemed to have become sterile or stationary. Both counselor and counselee, being reminded of the reality of the relationship of the "Wonderful Counselor," have been encouraged to continue their search for the best solution.

I could give many illustrations of the effectiveness of this approach in dealing with "nominal Christians" or those who made no claim to a Christian profession. When Edith came for an interview, she told me that she had no active interest in any church. The church had failed her, she felt, in an hour of need. I thought I sensed bitterness in her voice.

In the initial interview it was evident that Edith was having real difficulty in restraining her tears. Eventually she was overcome, and for some minutes she could only cry. This was even before she began to tell me her problem. When she regained control of herself she expressed anxiety and hostility toward members of her family. "Well, that's the story," she concluded.

"I can see that you have a serious and deep-seated problem," I said, "and from the compulsiveness of your weeping I am wondering if I have any right to try to help you, instead of referring you to a psychiatrist."

"I won't go to a psychiatrist," was her immediate response. "But I hoped you could help me."

"Of course I will do my best. I recognize from what I have seen and heard that your problem and your emotional condition should probably be dealt with by someone more competent than I am—a psychiatrist."

No, she assured me, she would not see a psychiatrist. Unless I would work with her, she would call this the end of our relationship.

It was then that I said, "Well, I believe very sincerely that all of us are limited in what we can do for others under such conditions, but I have not the slightest doubt that there is One who knows the answers. He has promised to guide us if we will humbly seek His guidance. He is the Holy Spirit."

Immediately I could see she was receptive to this idea. New light in her face suggested that she now had some hope of help.

As the weeks and months passed, though, we were often discouraged. I wondered if any progress was being made. Yet I could begin to see a few changes in her attitude. She no longer had the compulsive crying spells.

Then one day she said, "You know, you seemed to really believe what you said that day when you referred to the Holy Spirit being the Wonderful Counselor who is ready, willing, and able to provide the wisdom we needed for solving my problem."

"Yes, indeed I do," I said, "and without this faith I think I would not have had the courage to work with you or with many others whose problems are certainly beyond my ability, apart from His guidance."

As little by little I was led to help Edith, she, in turn, showed an increasing interest in God. One day she asked me, "What is necessary to become a member of the church of which you are a member?" I explained the requirements to her but added, "Why do you ask this?"

"Because I can see that you believe what you say and that it works," was her reply. "If the church means this much to you, I see no reason why it should not and could not to me."

As a result, Edith joined the church and became one of the most active and faithful members in the remaining years of my stay in that city. And following my departure, I heard from her on special occasions, as she reported on her active interest in the church and the Christian faith.

This, to me, was an experience of regeneration through counseling. I wonder if it would have taken place had I not been confident of the presence, power, and wisdom of the Holy Spirit and His availability to help. Most certainly I would never have been able to open the door to the spiritual realm of Edith's life had I not been confident of the reality and power of God working through His Holy Spirit.

Sometimes the Holy Spirit seems to work very rapidly as in Sarah's case. Apparently one reference to the Christian principle of doing good in return for evil brought about a change in both a marriage relationship and a relationship between in-laws. In Edith's case, the process was slower, running over several months of weekly interviews. Such differences may not always be explainable, though here it was partly due to using a different approach for Edith than for Sarah.

With Sarah I used confrontation counseling. With Edith it was more in the nature of supportive counseling. During interview after interview, I gave Edith opportunity to ventilate her hostilities and fears, and at the same time I provided reassurance and support. This was the normal way in which to restore Edith's faith as she watched and sometimes tested the consistency and genuineness of my own faith. In turn I reminded her from time to time of the presence and work of the Holy Spirit. That Edith needed supportive counseling was indicated by her crying, which is a method used by an infant to gain attention, recognition, or some other form of help from the parent. Following this clue, I gave her every opportunity to unburden herself and to tell in detail, sometimes with a degree of repetition, the things that had hurt her in her relationship with her siblings.

With both Edith and Sarah, my aim was to have patience and understanding mingled with compassion and love. This attitude was especially important in Edith's case, because she was quite overweight. She had a rather long history of being obese and feeling unwanted and unloved. She had craved understanding, acceptance, and appreciation from her parents and siblings, and when she did not get this love, as she felt, she increasingly craved it from other people. In her more recent years she had craved this affirmation from her husband, but he had been unable, apparently, to give it to her, partly because of her physical condition.

Let me relate another incident in which I feel the Holy Spirit was able to work regeneration in the counselee through me. Lorraine was a deeply depressed person whom I would have readily referred to a psychiatrist had she been willing and able to go to one. But she was not. So relying upon the Holy Spirit for His guidance and for His use of all the knowledge and ability I had, I began a long continuing series of interviews stretching over five or six years.

During those years I often saw little or no improvement, and sometimes I felt Lorraine was deteriorating in her effort to improve. Again and again she would revert to the same expression of guilt feelings which began in her childhood and were intensified in her adolescent years when, through some questionable experiences, she became convinced that she was totally lost and had committed the unpardonable sin.

When she came for counseling she was tremendously rigid,

almost hopelessly depressed, tense, extremely nervous, very much underweight, and was never able to smile regardless of the occasion. Her usual position in the interview was sitting erect on the front edge of her chair, and her facial expression seldom varied from the solemn sad expression of one who considered herself lost and doomed with no hope for the future.

Again and again I asked for the Holy Spirit's guidance, and time after time we discussed God's mercy and love. I assigned her readings and studies to emphasize and clarify the mercy and love of God and His willingness and eagerness to forgive through Christ. None of this seemed to have the slightest effect on her, for she would come in at each succeeding interview with the same sad depression and sense of hopelessness.

Lorraine's religious background did not help her overcome this extremely negative attitude. She was brought up in a theologically rigid denomination whose preachers constantly emphasized man's sinfulness and guilt in the sight of God, and God's judgment, ultimate punishment, and condemnation upon sinners. God could never be a God of love to Lorraine, and even if He were He could never love one such as she. The only logical approach for me to take seemed to be patient listening and frequent reassurance of God's love, using both illustrations and Scripture references to point out God's desire, willingness, and ability to forgive sinners—even the chief of sinners—and to wipe out their sins forever for Christ's sake.

But Lorraine was convinced within herself that she was not only lost but that her life was useless. I tried to discover and point out to her every possible potential for usefulness she had, whether through her education or her talents and abilities, many of which were completely undeveloped and unrecognized.

On one occasion, rather early in our relationship, it became clear that Lorraine was finding it very difficult to express orally the deeper feelings and fears of her mind and heart, so I suggested that she jot down such thoughts during the interval between interviews and bring in her notes. This she readily agreed to do, and at each succeeding interview she brought in many pages carefully written in long hand, relating her experiences of the week and describing her feelings about herself and her relationship to her husband, daughter, and others. All her feelings were primarily negative.

But as time went on I noticed that her ability to express herself in writing was extraordinarily clear, and that it was done with a careful choice of words and an unusually good vocabulary. I knew that she had a Master's Degree and had at one time been a teacher, which helped explain these abilities. I commented on them to Lorraine, and encouraged her to consider using her writing for some constructive purpose such as writing notes to friends or acquaintances on special occasions or in times of joy or sorrow.

I had a dual purpose in my suggestion. I wanted to help her realize that she had a talent which could be used effectively and to learn that there were people who needed the kind of support and encouragement which she might supply through its use. Focusing her attention more on others would turn her thoughts away from herself, developing in her more objectivity and reducing her subjectivity. This idea seemed to come to me from above through the Holy Spirit's guidance. But it was only the beginning.

In one interview I asked her if she had ever done much writing. She said, rather timidly, that she had liked to write verse but had never made any use of it. When I asked her if she would like to let me see some of what she had written, it was evident that this pleased and flattered her. I suggested that she bring it in on her next appointment.

I found the verse so well expressed and so thoughtful that I commended her very highly for it. Later on I made it possible for her to meet and talk with two different writers who were local members of the Pen Women's Guild. One of these had written for publications in her own denomination. The other was a poetess who had published a number of books of verse and was nationally known. Lorraine was hesitant about making the contacts—she was self-conscious, timid, and self-deprecating—but additional support finally encouraged her to make the contacts.

Both writers commended her verse highly and gave her suggestions by which she could improve her writing so that some of it might be published. Later she did have some of her verse published in her denominational publications, and when a special historical celebration was approaching in her church she wrote an extended script of the history in verse. This was so well done that her church used it on the anniversary occasion, thus giving her special recognition and attention.

Another suggestion I made was, I believe, directly from the Holy Spirit. It resulted from Lorraine's comment that she had never learned how to be a good homemaker or housewife. She didn't know how to cook, and she felt very inadequate when it came to entertaining anyone in her home. She knew nothing about sewing or any of the other domestic arts. I suggested that she go to the library and see the librarian. I had previously talked to the librarian, requesting her help in giving Lorraine some specific books and materials which would teach her both how to cook and how to sew. Being a good student and anxious to improve, Lorraine followed my suggestions and read the books. Because she was quite capable, she developed remarkable skill both in cooking and sewing, and finally began to feel much easier about inviting friends in for meals.

Before this improvement occurred, however, Lorraine had withdrawn from almost all social contact including attendance at her church and teaching a Bible class. Gradually she became more confident in the domestic area and accepted this as a part of God's will for her life. It was now clear that she was making progress. This progress, while slow, was nonetheless consistent. Little by little she became more and more relaxed, less anxious, more self-accepting, and ready and willing to believe that God could and would accept her as His child.

The end results were so rewarding that, as the years have passed, she has kept in touch with me even though we now live in different states. She never allows a special occasion or anniversary to occur without writing some verse for me or my wife appropriate for the occasion. She is interested and active in both her church and community.

Another and different type of counseling situation arose when a prominent and capable businessman in his late forties or early fifties called and made an appointment saying that he needed to see me immediately and that he was in serious difficulty. Arthur was a very prominent stock broker who had been instrumental in serving as the advisor and representative of many clients, making investments for them in the stock market. His reputation was above reproach as a businessman, and his integrity was unquestioned. But now he was in trouble. His depression was so great he was seriously considering suicide. Up to this time his relationship to the church had been purely a nominal one, as had his wife's, and they were living in such financial affluence that I had assumed they felt little or no need to rely on God or be active in the church.

But now, because of a crisis, and knowing nowhere else to turn, Arthur had come to the pastoral counselor in the church of which he was a member. What could he do? He had disappointed and perhaps financially ruined his best friends whose funds he had invested in what he thought would be blue chip stock investments. He himself had put most of his own money in this particular stock. Suddenly, however, the company apparently had failed, and all seemed to be lost.

As Arthur saw it, he was disgraced, a failure, had ruined his friends, and now there was little or no chance of his son ever receiving the fine education they had planned for him. Besides this, he was humiliated because his wife was having to look for a job at this time in life when she ought to have been able to relax and enjoy the income he would have provided had he used better judgment. Just what could I do to help him under these conditions?

Frankly, I did not know. But I was convinced that there was One who did know and who could open the way, though it seemed very dark and impossible from the human standpoint.

I began by mentioning the fact that human beings are very limited in their knowledge and foresight, and that all of us are subject to mistakes. Surely Arthur did not deliberately pick a failing stock, nor was the failure proof at all of his lack of good judgment. Circumstances beyond his control or knowledge had brought about this difficulty, and he could not be held responsible. It might have happened to anyone at any time, and he must admit and acknowledge this fact. Intellectually, Arthur agreed with my analysis, but emotionally he could not accept it, for his guilt feelings were so vivid and powerful that all else seemed to be of little consequence.

As on many other occasions when I completely lacked knowledge of the next step, I silently sent up "flash prayers" that the Holy Spirit would show me what to say and what to do next.

In answer, the next thought that came was to ask Arthur how his wife felt about all this. He replied that Ella was quite willing to work and that she was trying her best to share the burden with him and relieve him of his anxiety. But her willingness made him feel more guilty and less worthwhile. Would he be willing for Ella to come in to see me, I asked, either with him or without him. He readily agreed, and we arranged an appointment for the two of them to come together at the earliest possible time because of the urgency of the situation.

When they came, I asked Ella to express how she felt about the situation and what she saw with regard to the future. Her response was so spontaneous and wholehearted that her husband could hardly doubt her sincerity, nor could I. She was not despairing at all, nor did she even seem depressed. Rather, her face and voice indicated that she regarded this as a challenge which might draw them closer together and would give her the feeling that she could make some worthwhile contribution. Her willingness to work was evident, and it seemed possible that she could help her husband in his office, reducing his office expense, and enabling him to save some money.

This provided a small degree of encouragement for Arthur, but it was mixed with that same feeling of guilt—if he had shown better judgment his wife would never have had to come to the rescue. He seemed to feel that he had failed as a man and as a provider. But on this point no one could have provided more reassurance than Ella. She rose nobly to the occasion and with such conviction and spontaneity that I believe even he began to be convinced.

This was the last interview we had for some months, for it was the last one needed. In an amazing way the Holy Spirit seemed to take over and become the Counselor, saving Arthur's pride and restoring some of his self-respect—he no longer had to lean upon a human counselor. He and his wife were drawn closer together in a more intimate relationship than they had known for years.

The next time I saw Arthur he seemed to be a different man. He and Ella returned to the church with a more active interest than they had had for many years. Arthur readily acknowledged that God was working wonders, and that the situation apparently was not so hopeless as it had first appeared. He found that a portion of the apparent loss would not occur and that there was a possibility that in the end, over a longer period of time, little or nothing might be lost. He gave God the credit for this change which seemed to him to be little less than a miracle, as it did to me.

I feel that the end result was a regeneration of this man and his wife on the spiritual level, saving them from undue reliance upon material things and human judgment. It made them keenly aware of their need for God and His guidance in their daily lives and in the business in which he was engaged.

Still another instance comes to mind in connection with the regenerative function of the Holy Spirit operating through the pastoral counselor. A young man in his senior year in a university made an appointment for counseling. I knew that Terry was a very charming and delightful person who made plans instantly and whom the average person would never have thought of as being depressed or anxious. But as he sat in my office the first moments were almost silent ones. Then, to my complete surprise, he put his head in his hands and began to sob. I made no effort to stop his release of emotional tension, and in a few moments he regained his composure and was ready to talk.

As I recall, his first words, were, "I'm not fit to live."

"Of course you must feel very deeply about this," I responded, "but I have no idea why you feel this way and wonder if you wish to share your feelings with me."

He had been very much in love, Terry told me, and was ready to marry this fine girl but, as in several other cases, when he felt drawn to a girl he reached this point and had to ruin it all.

"Ruin it all?" I asked.

"Yes, every time I get to this point with a truly fine girl I feel that I must confess to her my unworthiness, and of course this would be the end of any possibility of marriage."

"Would you care to explain why you feel so unworthy?"

"Yes," he said. "It's hard, but I'll try."

"I believe you said you felt you're not fit to live."

"Yes, that's true, and the reason is that I am a victim of a terrible habit, the habit of masturbation, and I seem totally unable to break it. I know this is one of the most terrible of sins, and I feel that I am lost. In the past I have felt strongly that I ought to go into the ministry, and God could use me there if I were only fit, but of course I'm not."

Once more, as a "flash prayer" went up for the Holy Spirit's guidance, the answer seemed to come instantly.

"Why do you think this is so great a sin?" I asked. "Where did you get your idea?"

"Well, isn't it?"

"You seem to feel it is," I said, "but I want to know where you got your information."

"From the Bible, I suppose," he replied.

"Would you mind pointing out to me the passage or passages which state, indicate, or even imply that this is a sin?"

"Well, really I can't right now," he said, "but I am sure there are many passages to that effect."

"Well, maybe so," I responded, "but I really don't know any of them. Do you have a complete concordance?"

"Yes."

"Suppose, then, between now and our next interview you make a list of every reference that has to do directly or indirectly, by statement or implication, with this particular thing as a great sin and bring it in to me so we can discuss it."

Terry readily agreed to this assignment and went out feeling confident that he could produce such a list.

But on his next appointment, Terry looked rather nonplussed when I asked for the list. "You know, I just haven't been able to find anything that applies, but I am sure there is much about it in the Bible."

"Well," I told him, "I have never been able to put my finger on it, and I had hoped you would, so that we would know what it says. Maybe you had better continue looking and bring in this list the next time you come."

With that, the second interview was closed and the date and hour set for the next one.

"I'll just have to give up," Terry told me at his third appointment. "I can't find any references at all, unless the one about Onan's spilling his seed on the ground has to do with it."

Without going into detail, I reminded him that this had

nothing to do with masturbation, but that the sin here was the refusal to comply with the Old Testament law of "levirate marriage" which required a man to produce an heir to his deceased brother by the widow.

As I spoke, the expression on Terry's face changed from anxiety and fear and guilt to one of relief. He seemed suddenly to be set free. He was then ready to talk further about his future plans and vocation as a minister. Perhaps he could ask this fine girl with whom he was in love to marry him! Maybe God could use him in the ministry! Here was every evidence of a regenerated person; he came in as a doomed person and went out after this interview a new and happy man.

When such major changes in lives are possible as a result of this simple effort to introduce the spiritually regenerative power of the Holy Spirit, it is sad that pastor-counselors sometimes overlook the opportunity or fail to follow the leads counselees give us. The Holy Spirit is a rich resource and brings an unspeakably rich reward for counselor and counselee alike. Surely we need to become alert to our opportunities and more skillful in doing regenerative counseling! Time and eternity will provide unspeakable satisfaction and joy if we make the wisest and best possible use of our God-given opportunities in the realm of the spirit.

11.   ACHIEVING
MATURITY

><<<<<<<<<<<<<<<<<<<<<<<<<<<<<<<<<<<<<<<<<<<<<<<<<<<<

I have come that men may have life, and may have it
in all its fullness.
> —JOHN 10:10, *New English Bible*

So shall we all at last attain to the unity inherent in our
faith and our knowledge of the Son of God—to mature
manhood, measured by nothing less than the full stat-
ure of Christ.
> —EPHESIANS 4:13, *New English Bible*

Eva had been very popular. Several times in the past she had
been "sure" she was in love and had become engaged. But each
time she had discovered she was mistaken and had broken the
engagement. This time, however, was "different!" She was "certain" of this!

Since there were many factors which would suggest difficult

or impossible adjustments between Eva and Jim if this marriage were to work out, many of Eva's friends and relatives showed little enthusiasm for the prospective marriage. This, together with her own secret uncertainty, led Eva to withdraw from friends and family for some weeks.

During this time she felt compelled to seek counseling help from a Christian counselor whom she trusted. He was sympathetic, accepting, analytical, and wisely objective. He helped her to look at her relationship to Jim (as well as to the others to whom she had formerly been engaged), in the light of emotional maturity. She gained new insights, came to recognize and admit (in tears) that she needed to "grow up," and sincerely asked for help.

As weeks passed into months, Eva showed more and more signs of maturing. She broke the engagement to Jim because she now realized "that Jim is not for me and I would not be good for him." Having reached this conclusion, Eva became more relaxed, more responsible, more stable. Occasional visits with the counselor served the useful purpose of helping her to see her progress and to plan future steps in growth.

In the quotations at the head of the chapter, the Christian pastor has set before him both the goal of maturity and the assurance for helping his counselees achieve it. Achieving maturity is a slow process usually, though sometimes it may be sudden, the result perhaps of some traumatic experience or crisis above which one is able to rise to the degree that he is becoming a mature person. When they are properly understood and coped with, crises are escalators to growth.

For the pastoral counselor to aid a person in this process of growth toward maturity, he must first recognize certain facts about human beings. Many have stated the ultimate importance of the spiritual factor in achieving maturity. Plato said it this way: "If the head and body are to be well, you must begin by curing the soul." Since we are concerned about helping counselees achieve maturity, it seems that the wisest beginning point is the realm of the spiritual. Here, as in other aspects of personality, there are hindrances to growth which definitely block progress. In this deeper spiritual realm these blocks are more clearly related to man's relationship to God—a relationship basically inseparable from the relationship to his fellow man. We recognize the impossibility of loving God while hating our brother; the person who claims he can actually have this intimate and warm relationship with God while holding within him hostility and unforgiveness toward his fellow man is deceiving himself (I John 4:20–21).

Among the hindrances to growth are anxiety, hostility, envy, self-centeredness, fear, jealousy, or any negative or destructive attitudes toward oneself or others. All of these separate a person from the source of that strength which is essential to growth. The removal of such blocks is essential to ultimate attainment of maturity. Though we believe the ability to overcome these must come from God Himself as we rely upon Him in faith, nevertheless the pastoral counselor has a distinct function in aiding his counselee in this direction.

Counseling techniques can help a person achieve insight so that the blocks are uncovered and become clear to him. Seeing them thus clearly as direct hindrances to growth seems to be the first essential in coping with them. In this process one of the most effective methods is confrontation. Having identified the difficulty and helped his counselee to recognize its nature, the counselor confronts the counselee with both the destructiveness of this blockage and the possibilities of removing it. No counselor can do this until he himself has attained an experiential knowledge of these possibilities within himself. But knowing from first-hand experience that obstacles can be overcome, he can speak with conviction. This assurance strengthens a person's confidence in the competence of the counselor and helps him take the next step under the counselor's guidance—that is to set and work toward a goal.

A number of psychologists and others have listed the criteria of maturity. I have chosen to follow the list set up by one of our most outstanding psychologists, Gordon W. Allport, in his recent volume entitled *Pattern and Growth in Personality.*[1] He lists six such criteria which I shall take in turn and illustrate with real case histories.

1. EXTENSION OF THE SELF

Ruth was a very capable person in her early forties. She was attractive, intellectual, and capable as a wife and mother. But since her children were now pretty much on their own, she was not needed as a mother in the old sense. Her husband had taken over the two boys, and she felt alone and rejected. The boys were not courteous to her or considerate of her, and her husband was very indulgent with them.

Ruth became greatly depressed. Over a long period of counseling she seemed to make very little progress, though the sources of her depression were largely ferreted out and found to be in her unfulfilled feminine needs. She had lost her self-confidence, had become quite critical and almost bitter toward her husband, and spent most of her time brooding over her unhappy and unfortunate life.

At this stage—when she had gained insight but was still very unhappy and saw little or no hope for the future—I was able to point out to her that when a person's focus is entirely subjective, as hers was, life is hardly worth living and one actually settles down to a bare and meager existence. I pointed out to her the necessity of finding some significant way to extend herself.

In her college days, Ruth had been a good student with a major in mathematics. She still had a great interest in the subject though she had little use to put it to. One day I asked her if she had ever thought of going back and taking a refresher course at the university to prepare for teaching mathematics. I

[1] New York: Holt, Rinehart and Winston, 1961.

suggested the scarcity of math teachers in the community and the increasing need for well-prepared teachers in this subject for high school students.

Her attention was caught by the idea, and after some weeks of investigation she found that she could be admitted to the university for refresher work and that there was a possibility of securing a job on the faculty of a high school nearby. These possibilities seemed to give her the necessary incentive to act on the suggestion. As she attended classes for special study and met other people in the same field, there was a marked change in her attitude both toward herself and toward her family.

Ruth did so well in her studies in fact that her whole family was proud of her. Her oldest son, who had now finished college, became so proud of his mother that he told others about her and her ability. This pleased her greatly and foretold the beginning of a new, more mature phase of life.

All of this was a step in the right direction, but it was not enough, since Ruth's spiritual development was also arrested, partly because of her older son's rebellion against the church as he knew it. But with his changed attitude toward her accomplishments she turned back to the church which had once meant much to her.

This turn came when she was invited to teach a special course in the church school. Feeling that she was now once more accepted and appreciated by her family, she accepted the invitation gladly and did an outstanding job.

As Ruth began to extend herself intellectually and spiritually, her home situation was greatly improved, she began to mature, and life took on new meaning. Maturing through extending self is a part of the growth process, and the counseling pastor can play an important part in aiding growth by suggesting ways for people to extend themselves. He has access both to the individuals who make up his congregation and to an ongoing program of education and character development which the church is equipped to provide.

2. WARM RELATING OF SELF TO OTHERS

Maturation requires that individuals be able to relate to others in a warm and intimate way. This intimate relationship is not confined to the sexual relationship between husband and wife, as some writers seem to think, but it applies also to other interpersonal relationships as well. Dr. Allport says that "this type of warmth may be called *compassion*."

The case of Mrs. Lawrence illustrates this aspect of growth. She came for counseling because she felt her home and her selfhood were "falling apart," and she had lost the zest for living. She was a person with great potential—a very feminine woman as well as a leader of uncommon capacity. But she felt that she was no longer able to fulfill either role.

Mr. Lawrence seemed no longer to understand her needs or to care for her companionship. He was completely absorbed in his work and in his children. He did not need her and she was now unable to respond to him sexually. She felt so unnecessary as a woman and as a person that she had resigned from some community activities in which she was formerly interested. She no longer felt adequate even to work in her church. Her plight was pathetic and she was approaching a state of bitterness and cynicism.

If Mrs. Lawrence was to be helped it seemed essential for me to work with her husband also. Would he come? Mrs. Lawrence told him of her need for help and that I had suggested that I could do very little to help her unless I had his assistance. He readily agreed to come, since he, too, was very unhappy about their marriage relationship.

As counseling proceeded it became clear that Mr. Lawrence had decided several years before to give more time to his children. They were rapidly growing up and he hardly knew them. So he began to take more and more time and interest in them and their activities. This became increasingly satisfying to him even to the point that they were allowed to absorb a larger portion of his time and attention than he was giving to his wife. But he did not realize how Mrs. Lawrence was beginning to feel about this, becoming more and more jealous of his attention and more and more resentful toward her children.

As her reaction to her husband's neglect increased in intensity, and she felt less and less needed as a wife and mother, Mrs. Lawrence's interest in and ability to respond sexually became almost nonexistent. She also reasoned that if she was such a failure as a wife and mother, she was certainly unfit to help others, either in church activities or in community services. It was then that she came to me for help.

In counseling Mr. Lawrence, I gradually helped him to understand what had been happening to his wife and therefore to their marriage. Being a very intelligent person and wanting very much to have a happy marriage and home life, he was very cooperative and began to change his focus of attention from the children back to his wife.

As a part of his effort to recover and improve the situation, Mr. Lawrence became active in the church and was elected to the official board. As they began to attend their church together, their spiritual interests grew stronger and stronger, and in their church life they found new depths of intimacy and enjoyment.

Gradually, also, Mrs. Lawrence felt accepted and needed by her husband and decided that she was not, after all, necessarily a failure as a woman. She became more and more perceptive and compassionate toward her husband, children, and the people with whom she came into contact in the church and community. Mrs. Lawrence was developing this second criteria of maturity —the ability to be warm in relating of her self to others.

3. EMOTIONAL SECURITY (SELF-ACCEPTANCE)

The ability to feel emotionally secure comes with self-acceptance. One who cannot accept himself as a real person finds himself in a constant state of uncertainty and therefore is unable to live a self-disciplined and balanced life. He is constantly anxious and strives to secure attention and win acceptance from others by devious emotional means. He overreacts to situations. He has temper outbursts of profanity and obscenity. He acts like a child rather than an adult. He meets daily demands upon him with temper tantrums, complaining, blaming others, and self-pity. He seems to feel that "every pinprick to his pride is a mortal wound." What can the pastor-counselor or friend do to help such persons to become self-accepting and mature?

Miss Bradley came in great distress for help. She had committed "the unpardonable sin" she said—and she seemed to be convinced of this. Actually, she did not have the slightest idea what that "sin" might be, but she was guilty of committing it!

I found that she was a minister's daughter, but for years she had had absolutely nothing to do with the church or religion. Her parents had failed her. She had never married and was now approximately sixty years old.

To add to her misery and misfortune it had fallen to her lot to live with and take care of her invalid, widowed sister for the past twenty years—and she didn't like it. Her hostility was very evident to the whole neighborhood, and especially to the children who at times dared to play on her lawn or near by. She would scream and hurl profane words at them as she drove them away.

Recently, however, the doctors had discovered that Miss Bradley had a terminal malignancy and must soon be hospitalized permanently. What could she do? God was punishing her for her rejection of Him. Her guilt was overwhelming and she must be doomed to an eternal hell. Her time was growing short, so her visit to me was a cry for help.

I felt this was no time to increase her sense of guilt, which was already unbearably painful. What she needed was to face the future with some kind of hope. I must find a way to do this. So I began by a reevaluation of God as a God of love—not of hate. I used many illustrations and Scripture references to show her this, and she seemed as receptive and eager as a little child.

Many hours, illustrations, and quotations later she accepted herself as one whom God looked upon as His child. His loving concern for her, as seen in Christ, finally got through to her mind and heart alike. Relief and joy showed on her face and in her voice. Now, in return for His acceptance and pardon she asked what she could possibly do out of her love and gratitude for Him.

In a counseling interview one day, Miss Bradley had mentioned two friends of hers whom she hadn't seen for years but to whom she once was very close. Her immaturity and hostile attitudes of recent years had separated them. Years ago they had left their church and would respond to no efforts of pastor or fellow parishioners to reenlist them.

With her new-found faith and joy, Miss Bradley suddenly said that perhaps she might help them to work through their hostility and bring about reconciliation between them and the church. I felt this was the prompting of the Holy Spirit and therefore encouraged her in every way possible to undertake this venture. The result was that the two became the active members they had been once before.

With this success and experience of joy behind her, Miss Bradley began giving more and more of her time to visiting and encouraging others in the neighborhood. But soon, as predicted, she had to be hospitalized. Accepting the inevitable, she seemed to be determined to be the most considerate and understanding patient in her ward. Her pain, while intense, only made her more concerned about other patients. Her thoughtfulness and expressed appreciation of the nurses and doctors during that last year of her life brought tears and compassion to the doctors and nurses who knew her. When I arrived at the hospital the morning of her death, I found her hospital room was full of doctors and nurses with tear-stained eyes.

Here a most immature and insecure person grew up to become an unusually mature person during the last years of her life.

4. REALISTIC PERCEPTION, SKILLS, AND ASSIGNMENTS

A mature person will be in close touch with reality. He will see things, people, and situations for what they are. He will have important work to do and therefore will learn and use skills to accomplish that work. This person has purpose and sees meaning in his life and keeps busy achieving that purpose. Idleness and hopeless despair are foreign to his habit of life. There is direction and dedication to his life's purpose, and his days and years are marked by accomplishment.

D. A. was a very intelligent, well-educated minister in a small, racially biased town in the deep south. He was restless, unhappy, frustrated, and seriously considering leaving the ministry. What was the use? His congregation was set in its ways and wouldn't hear what he was saying about the necessity for the Christian people of the community to have a broad and accepting attitude toward all people of all races. Why waste his life, training, and talents on a church like this? Surely, there were churches whose congregations were more responsive and less prejudiced!

When he came to me for counseling, D. A. was both discouraged and ready to give up. He was the victim, as I saw it, of a degree of emotional immaturity. He could not see objects, people, or situations for what they were. So we would begin there.

First of all I suggested he become a participating member of a small group that was involved in group dynamics. To this he readily agreed, for he had some knowledge of the possible values which might accrue to individuals through this interplay of mind and emotions under proper leadership. Over a series of weeks and months, D. A. was faithful in his attendance and participation in this group.

In addition we arranged some private interviews and later, when he had to go back to his church in another state, we continued our counseling through a frequent exchange of letters. During this process I repeatedly reminded him of his basic concern for the welfare and growth of people. There could be no denying of this. It was to this end that he had trained at seminary and entered the ministry. In addition, he had shown such ability as a student that he won a scholarship to study abroad, and had received his Ph.D. from a leading European university.

Through the years of study he was motivated by concern for people and their plight in our modern world. But now that he was "in" that world, he could see little response to his efforts.

I called to his attention some realities which he seemed to be overlooking. He had unusual training for this ministry. He had deep concern for people. He was willing to work to that end. But at this point he had regressed into a state of self-pity and hostility which were qualities of immaturity, as he well knew intellectually. It was my aim to bring this knowledge into full realization and to sharpen his perception, so that he could apply his skills in fulfilling his God-given assignment in the southern parish. Would he run away like a child in the face of difficulty? Or would he accept the people with whom he worked as persons who needed the skills and perception and efforts he would put forth? These were questions with which I confronted D. A. and to which he gradually but genuinely responded.

Eventually D. A. wrote that he had discovered he was needed where he was. He felt the challenge of working through the difficulties, no matter how long this might take. His tension, impatience, and frustration seemed to grow dim and finally vanish. We both agreed that he was much more mature as a result of the counseling experience.

5. SELF-OBJECTIFICATION: INSIGHT AND HUMOR

Dr. Allport quotes Santayana as saying, "Nothing requires a rarer intellectual heroism than willingness to see one's equation written out." This is also one of the criteria of maturity, according to Dr. Allport. It is the ability to see oneself objectively with all one's incongruities and absurdities. It is a matter of having true insight and being able to laugh at one's infantile conduct without rejecting one's self.

W. Burney Overton, a competent pastor-counselor and a close friend of mine, tells of a case which clearly illustrates this kind of situation. Jim, who was in his middle forties, came to Burney for counseling. His problem was that he was finding it difficult to dissociate himself from a much younger woman, even though he was married.

Early in the counseling process Jim spoke of his ambivalent feelings toward his father. He had wanted desperately to be accepted and approved by his father while all but hating him for his near-sadistic treatment of him. His father (now dead for a number of years) used to "tease" him by offering a close, affectionate relationship, then withdrawing just when Jim thought he might really be loved by his father.

The young woman in whom he had become emotionally interested and whom he wanted to "forget," was one who also teased him by making him feel that she loved him, until he reached out in response to that "love." Then she would withdraw, leaving him frustrated and hostile.

As the counseling relationship was strengthened, Burney said to Jim, "Tell me once more about your father and how he treated you."

As Jim retold the story, suddenly insight came. "That's the same way this girl treats me, isn't it?"

Yes, Burney responded. Jim was mistaking the girl for his father. Imagine the ludicrous and impossible situation this presented. Jim, the middle-aged man, had reacted to this young girl just as if she were his father! Jim saw the ridiculousness of this identification and actually laughed at himself. So Jim became more mature—he was objective to the point that he could look at himself in this relationship and see the humor of it all.

6. THE UNIFYING PHILOSOPHY OF LIFE

Maturity, according to Allport, requires also a clear comprehension of life's purpose in terms of an understandable theory. One must have some form of unifying philosophy of life, and a worthy goal toward which to direct his life's thoughts and efforts.

A young minister came in for counseling because he had almost "cracked up" in his boss's office. Al was on the church staff of a prominent downtown church in a southern city, having completed his seminary training only a year and a half previously. He said that he was in his superior's office trying to plan with him when suddenly he could control his feelings no longer. He broke down and cried.

Back of this outbreak was an accumulation of frustration coupled with hostility toward his superior. Every idea or suggestion he made in line with his interest and skills was turned down. Al felt life had no meaning. What use was there in merely "running a machine" with little or no concern for people. And there were so many needy people all around the church who needed help! He had suggested that it might be helpful if he could rent an apartment near the church where the young people of the downtown area might "drop in" for a chat and thus give him an opportunity to minister to their needs. But the senior pastor felt that some of his church members might think the young minister didn't appreciate the "nice" home they provided for him in the "better section" of the city. No, that wouldn't do! And this was the last straw. There was no use!

In the counseling process I discovered that Al placed an unusually high value on people as people. The most important goal in his life was to reach people in need, wherever they lived. Programs and promotion seemed artificial and largely unrelated to life. But he was being compelled to spend his time as a cog in this "machine." Here was the root of his emotional outbreak, approaching a "breakdown."

My task was cut out for me—help this young man accurately evaluate his real motives, desires, talents, training. From there we must move on to discover possible ways in which he might fulfill these deeper, more personal needs to serve. So we examined various possibilities and came to a possible course of study which would prepare him for the more intimate, person-to-person ministry which he felt was essential, if his life was to be fulfilled and if he were to achieve the goals and values that had meaning for him.

In concluding this chapter, one more comment needs to be made—there is always suffering that accompanies maturation or growth toward maturity. The way we learn to handle suffering determines, in large measure, whether that suffering will become a deficit or an asset. If we accept suffering (though we never really want to suffer) as a potential challenge to growth, it can become just that. The moral and spiritual muscles which learn to endure suffering with patience, cannot be developed in any more definite ways.

The pastor-counselor or friend who understands this, and who learns from personal experience to look on suffering in this way, can open new doors toward maturity for counselees who without this insight might falter and fall under the weight of pain. Romans 5:3–5 is a very helpful Scripture at this point, and particularly in the Revised Standard Version can be a source of gaining insight as well as support. The same is true of I Corinthians 10:13. J. B. Phillips' translation clarifies and emphasizes the message of both portions.

Let me quote I Corinthians 10:13 from another translation —*Good News for Modern Man*—as the concluding word of this chapter, a word of strength and comfort:

Every temptation that has come your way is the kind that normally comes to people. For God keeps his promise, and he will not allow you to be tempted beyond your power to resist; but at the time you are tempted he will give you the strength to endure it, and so provide you a way out.

12. THE GOD
WE TRUST

~~~~~~

One of the deeper desires of our time seems to be the desire to find meaning—a practical and reasonable meaning that is intellectually acceptable in a busy, scientifically minded age such as this. One reason why so many seem to have lost interest in and loyalty to the established churches and their teachings is that many of these teachings need to be reexamined and restated in language that can be understood and is relevant to our present world.

A faith for today must "get to us," or as our young people say, the church and its preaching must "get with it." How can this be done in the realm of the religious or spiritual if our attempts to teach and preach are still geared to the thinking and orientation of the past century? We must not expect people of the younger generation to use or understand the meaning of "horse-and-buggy" analogies. They need teaching and terminology appropriate to the space age.

Our time is not primarily a time of the classic philosophers of the past. It is the day of the scientific mind and approach. The questions being asked today are not so much "By what authority?" but "How do you explain the relevancy of your teaching and preaching in terms of our space-age language and needs?" With this in mind, I am adding this final chapter to present some ideas which, to me, seem far more realistic, down-to-earth, and relevant than the traditional and formal declarations of past theologians.

Our concept of the basic nature of God—whom we have traditionally called "the Triune God"—is one which I feel needs such a restatement. Semantics are important to understanding and we have confused rather than clarified this concept by our choice of words. I refer, now, to the use of the word "persons" as applied to the nature of God. I much prefer to think of God as having three "major functions" or "facets" to His nature and being—God acts or functions as "Father," as "Son," and as the "Holy Spirit."

To clarify this view, when I think of God in His "Father" function or aspect, I think of Him as the head of His family in heaven and on earth. In this role as Father, He is the source and creator of all life, as well as the sustainer, maintainer, and protector of His vast family.

The word "family" is for me all-inclusive. It embraces the whole creation as it exists throughout time and space and eternity, both in the organic and inorganic, the physical and spiritual realms. The "fatherhood" concept of God has tremendous value for every individual, once it is understood. By this understanding I mean that He is a Father who is genuinely concerned for and loves all His creatures. That concern is completely adequate and inexhaustible and ever-accessible to all of His creation. His infinitude, eternity, and unchangeableness involve His very nature and substance. He is completely reliable as a Father to His children. His other attributes as Father are equally important and essential to our security and well-being.

Since He never grows old, weak, or changeable, and is never

absent or far removed from the least of us His children, the perfection of His other attributes is completely sufficient to satisfy all our needs. If we need wisdom, He is that wisdom; if we need strength or power, He is all powerful; if the frustrations resulting from sin call for holiness, His holiness is perfect and inexhaustible; if justice is our need, we can relax and be certain that the Judge of all the earth will never be unfair to the least of these little ones, His children; our deep and lasting need for love will be perfectly satisfied as His goodness and love follow us all the days of our lives. If we are toubled by falsehood, deception, and ignorance, we may turn confidently to Him who is "the Truth." And so we see God the Father as capable of meeting all our needs in life here and hereafter.

When God revealed Himself in the human form of Jesus Christ, He did so with a direct purpose for our good. No person can become mature or complete as God intends him to become until he learns to live with himself and with his fellows in vital relationship best demonstrated in the person of Christ who so loved each and every person that He gave His all for their redemption and reconciliation.

To show how this can be done, God the Father voluntarily and really took the role of "a son," and thus demonstrated for us our proper relationship to God the Father. Here, in Jesus of Nazareth we see a true man, living among men, in the workaday world with its trials, its joys, its sorrows, its temptations, but always living triumphantly as He humbly sought to know and do His Father's will. He so completely trusted His Father that life was not so precious to Him as obedience to the Father. And so we hear Him pleading that He might be spared "this cup" if possible, but at the same time pleading that His Father's will, rather than His, be done. Here is submission to the Father which God the Father deserves. In Christ we also see that those of us who follow Christ and accept God's will completely, will, like Him, be ultimately exalted.

There are other implications and meanings of sonship as God

revealed it through Christ, and if we were writing a theology, chapters could be written on this subject. Here, however, I am only concerned to draw a thumbnail sketch of the God we trust. I want to go on to consider the third function or aspect of God—the Holy Spirit.

We have already looked at the meaning of "spirit" as derived from the Hebrew and Greek words used in the Old and New Testaments. Here I want to point up in a few words the profound value of this aspect of God's nature to me and to others who counsel.

Jesus said that when He returned to the Father He would send the Holy Spirit to be the Comforter or Counselor to His disciples. It was to their advantage to have Him ever-present in their hearts, so that wherever they went and whatever they did they could never be separated from God the Holy Spirit who, because of his "spiritual" nature, could dwell within their hearts, to direct their minds and words under all conditions.

In any other form than that which we call "spirit," God could be separated from us, and the secret and unspoken cries of the heart would never be heard by Him. But since, as Jesus said, "when the Spirit comes, he shall abide in" our hearts, then He is never remote from us, but is ever present and ready to help. This has been a source of tremendous comfort and of practical assistance to me in the years that I have served as a pastor-counselor. Some of the instances given above are evidence of this but they could be multiplied many times from my files and from my memory.

My greatest debt, I feel, since my reconciliation to God by Christ on Calvary, is my debt to God the Holy Spirit. Therefore, to Him I dedicate this book with the earnest prayer that He may use it to His glory and to the benefit of countless readers.

FOR FURTHER READING

Bailey, Derrick Sherwin. *The Mystery of Love and Marriage.* New York: Harper & Bros., 1952.

Blanton, Smiley. *Love or Perish.* New York: Simon & Schuster, 1956.

Bruder, Ernest E. *Ministering to Deeply Troubled People.* Englewood Cliffs, N.J.: Prentice-Hall, Inc., 1963.

Clinebell, Howard J., Jr. *Basic Types of Pastoral Counseling.* Nashville: Abingdon Press, 1966.

Dicks, Russell L. *Pastoral Work and Personal Counseling.* New York: The Macmillan Co., 1945.

Drummond, Henry. *The Greatest Thing in the World.* Mount Vernon, N.Y.: Peter Pauper Press.

Duvall, Evelyn and Sylvanus. *Sex Ways in Fact and Faith.* New York: Association Press, 1961.

Fairchild, Roy W. *Christians in Families.* Richmond, Va.: CLC Press, 1964.

Fromm, Erich. *The Art of Loving.* New York: Harper & Bros., 1956.

Geiseman, O. A. *Make Yours a Happy Marriage.* St. Louis: Concordia Publishing House, 1946.

Howe, Reuel L. *The Creative Years.* Greenwich, Conn.: Seabury Press, 1959.

————. *Man's Need and God's Action.* Greenwich, Conn. Seabury Press, 1953.

————. *The Miracle of Dialogue.* Greenwich, Conn.: Seabury Press, 1963.

Hugen, M. D. *The Church's Ministry to the Older Unmarried.* Grand Rapids, Mich.: Wm. B. Eerdmans Publishing Co., 1960.

Johnson, Paul. *Christian Love.* New York: Abingdon-Cokesbury Press, 1951.

Marshall, Catherine. *Beyond Ourselves.* New York: McGraw-Hill Book Co., 1961.

May, Rollo. *Man's Search for Himself.* New York: W. W. Norton & Co., 1953.

Montagu, Ashley, editor. *The Meaning of Love.* New York: Julian Press, 1953.

Mosse, Eric P. *The Conquest of Loneliness.* New York: Random House, 1957.

Oates, Wayne, E., editor. *An Introduction to Pastoral Counseling.* Nashville: Broadman Press, 1959.

Phillips, J. B. *When God Was Man.* Nashville: Abingdon Press, 1955.

Pike, James A. *Beyond Anxiety.* New York: Charles Scribners Sons, 1953.

Snyder, Ross. *On Becoming Human.* New York: Abingdon Press, 1967.

Stewart, Charles William. *The Minister as Marriage Counselor.* Nashville: Abingdon Press, 1961.

Stolz, Karl R. *Making the Most of the Rest of Life.* New York: Abingdon-Cokesbury Press, 1941.

Tizard, Leslie J. and Harry J. S. Guntrip. *Middle Age.* Great Neck, N.Y.: Channel Press, 1960.

Tournier, Paul. *The Meaning of Persons.* New York: Harper & Bros., 1957.

Trueblood, Elton. *Your Other Vocation.* New York: Harper & Bros., 1952.

Weatherhead, Leslie D. *The Will of God.* New York: Abingdon Press, 1944.

Westberg, Granger E. *Good Grief.* Philadelphia: Fortress Press, 1962.